TEN STEPS

A consecutive, step-by-step understanding of the basics of the Christian fa

D1627169

Don Matzat

Good News Books
Wentzville, Missouri

Table of Contents

All Scripture references are from the *New International Version* of the Bible unless otherwise indicated.

Introduction:

On a trip I took to Egypt some years ago, I asked our Muslim guide to explain to our group what Islam was about. His explanation was very simple. All you had to do was believe there was one god, Allah, and Mohammed was his prophet; pray five times a day; fast during the holy month of Ramadan; give alms; and take a trip to Mecca, and some might add, Jihad or holy war. That was about it. Do those things and you are a good Muslim.

What does it mean to be a Christian? If that question was addressed to a group of "church-going Christians," you would probably get a wide variety of answers. Some would say a Christian is one who obeys the Ten Commandments. Others would identify a Christian as one who goes to Church and believes in the Bible. A man in a congregation I served in New York City identified a Christian as someone who is not a Jew. In his mind, if you're not one, you had to be the other. Of course, there would be some who would get the right answer and say that a Christian believes in Jesus and know their sins are forgiven because Jesus died for them, but I do believe they would be in the minority.

Some years ago, as a favor to the funeral director who happened to be a good friend, I did a funeral for a man I did not know. I asked the niece of the deceased whether her uncle was a Christian?

"Oh yes, he was a very good man," she confidently replied.

"I'm glad to hear he was a good man," I responded. "But was he a Christian?"

"Well," she thought. "I don't know if he went to church or owned a Bible or anything like that."

"Even so, that would not make him a Christian."

Being somewhat agitated, she asked, "Well, what is a Christian?"

"Someone who believes in Jesus Christ and knows that their sins are forgiven because Jesus died for them," I answered.

"Oh," she responded cynically. "I don't know anything about that."

A Christian is someone who believes in Jesus Christ and knows that their sins are forgiven because Jesus suffered and died for them. That is the simplest definition. The Cross, a Roman means of execution, is *the* Christian symbol. Christianity is about the forgiveness of sins.

Christianity is not about you. It is about what God has done for you. Both Islam and Judaism are based on what man does for God. Christianity is about what God has done for man. Jesus told his disciples that repentance and the forgiveness of sins will be preached to all nations. (Luke 24:47). When the Apostle Paul preached to the pagans in the Roman world, he declared the forgiveness of sins through Jesus Christ. While there are many today who are critical of Christianity and Christians in general, especially those who equate being a Christian with right-wing politics, how can anyone be against having their sins forgiven?

While the forgiveness of sins is at the heart and core of Christianity, there is a great deal of Christian teaching derived from Scripture which necessarily comes before and follows after. While every Christian Church or denomination recognizes the centrality of the Cross, the diversity exists in the "before and after" doctrines or teaching; how they are designed and where they are placed within the whole. I am writing from a Lutheran perspective, believing it is the correct interpretation of Scripture.

All Christian teaching is systematic. One truth is built upon that which has come before. It is like putting together an unassembled item. You are given step-by-step directions that must be precisely followed. You cannot begin Step 2 until you have completed Step 1. You will never fully grasp the impact of the forgiveness of sins until you first grasp the devastating results of sin.

Also, nothing can be thrown into the mix from "left-field" without being connected to the entire system. There are many strange teachings that are a part of fringe elements of Christianity. The question is, where do they fit?

The problem for most Christians is they come to church week after week and hear a variety of sermons dealing with different themes and topics and never put the whole thing together in a systematic fashion. That is my purpose in writing this book, to present a step-by-step understanding of basic Christian truth, building one truth upon the one that came before. You might think of it as Christianity 101. It of utmost importance that you consider each step carefully, embrace it, before moving on to the next.

"Questions for Discussion" are included after each chapter. A free "Instructor's Guide" is available. Request one by emailing me at donmatzat@hotmail.com.

May God richly bless your study of these "Ten Steps."

Dr. Donald G. Matzat
Wentzville, Missouri, 2018

Step 1:

I am not a sinner because I sin.
I sin, because I am a sinner.

My son and his family live in Parkland, Florida. My granddaughter Jenna was friends with several girls who went to Douglas High School where the massacre took place on Valentine's Day of 2018. Seventeen people were killed, mostly ninth grade children. Jenna was on a soccer team with Alyssa, a young lady who was one of the victims. They were very good friends. It is horrible to think that these children had to experience such absolute evil. Some of them will never get over it.

When you are confronted with the horrible things that take place in our world, you must ask the question, "What is wrong with people? Why do such things take place?"

There are numerous answers to that question.

Why Evil?

Some begin with the assumption that people are generally good but due to outside influences they may do bad things, even incredibly evil things. So, in dealing with perpetrators, the search goes on. What was in the background of Nikolas Cruz, the shooter, that caused him to do such a horrible thing? Was it an unstable family background? Did he play too many violent video games? Was he preoccupied with guns? The idea being that if you can remove all the outside influences you can eliminate the evil. Of course, if that were to happen, the only thing we would have left on television would be the Hallmark channel.

On the other hand, there are those who believe that we are a mixture of good and evil. In his inaugural address, Abraham Lincoln spoke of the "better angels of our nature." We have all probably seen the picture of the man with an angel on one shoulder telling him to be good and the devil on the other tempting him to do evil. Flip Wilson, a popular comedian some years ago, explained his bad behavior by saying, "The devil made me do it."

Christianity gets to the heart of the matter. In the Gospels, Jesus did not focus upon external behavior but upon the heart of the person. He said in Matthew 15:19: "For out of the heart come evil thoughts, murder, adultery, sexual immorality, theft, false testimony, slander." This emphasis of Jesus got him into trouble with the religious leaders of his day who prided themselves in their good works and holy living. Jesus referred to them as "whited tombs," they look good on the outside, but death reigned within.

In the same way, the Christian explanation of the human condition is not very popular in our world today. We preach and confess that people do the things they do because they have a corrupted human nature, and it all goes back to the sin of Adam. The Apostle Paul wrote in Romans 5:12: "Therefore, just as sin entered the world through one man, and death through sin, and in this way, death came to all men, because all sinned."

Original Sin

This human condition is called "original sin," or "inherited sin" originated with the sin of Adam. In Ephesians 2:1, the Apostle Paul speaks of man without Christ as being "dead in his transgressions and sins."

It is important to understand that human nature, including our will, emotion and intellect, is not corrupt but has been corrupt-ed by original sin. Human nature is a creation of God and is good. It is like rottenness getting into an apple. The apple is good, but it has been corrupted by rottenness.

Some years ago, a self-styled "pastor" led a small group of people into our community to form a little farming commune. We had lunch together, and he accused me of functioning out of my sinful nature because of the various programs I had developed in my congregation which were successful. He believed that the human will and intellect were corrupt and could not be used in the ministry. He said,

"We have to wait on God to act."

Well, they waited, and God never acted. They went broke and left.

In the life of a Christian, as we will see later, the Holy Spirit works through the will, emotions and intellect so that we might do the will of God.

Getting sin right is vitally important. If you get sin wrong, you will get everything wrong. Martin Luther wrote: "If you want to engage profitably in the study of theology and the Scripture and do not want to run head-on into a Scripture closed and sealed, then learn above all things, to understand sin aright."[1]

The primary confession of the churches of the Reformation, later identified as the Lutheran Church, is the *Augsburg Confession,* named as such because it was presented at the Diet or Assembly that met in 1530 in the city of Augsburg in Germany. The Confession defined what the Reformers believed and what they rejected. The first article of the Confession deals with the subject of God. The second article deals with original sin. The article states in part:

> *It is also taught among us that since the fall of Adam all men who are born according to the course of nature are conceived and born in sin. That is, all men are filled with evil lust and inclinations from their mother's*

---

[1] Ewald Plass, *What Luther Says,* (Saint Louis Concordia Publishing House, 1959) p.1295.

wombs and are unable by nature to have true fear of God and true faith in God.[2]

Martin Luther defined original sin as the evil inclination we find in ourselves to anger, hatred, unchastity, covetousness, glory, pride and the like.[3]

Lazarus Spengler, a prominent leader of the Reformation in Germany, wrote a hymn that was translated into English: "All Mankind Fell in Adam's Fall." The first stanza is: "All mankind fell in Adam's fall, one common sin infects us all; From sire to son the bane descends, and over all the curse impends."

When it comes to the subject of sin, the issue is not what we do but rather what we are. Every person born into this world is born in sin, or as David put it in Psalm 51:5: "Surely, I was sinful at birth, sinful from the time my mother conceived me." We are not sinners because we sin. Rather, we sin because we are sinners.

Born in Adam

We were all born "in Adam" or out of the root of Adam. What does this mean? How can we understand this?

---

[2] Theodore G. Tappert, *The Book of Concord,* (Philadelphia: Fortress Press, 1959), p. 29
[3] Plass, op.cit, p. 1296

Let's say your Great, Great Grandfather was run over and killed by a horse and buggy, what would have happened to you. You would have died *in him.* Or, as Marty McFly discovered in *Back to the Future,* if he was unable to bring his Father and Mother together at the school dance, he was being erased from the picture. What happened in the past affected his future.

One of the interesting illustration of what it means to be born "in Adam" is recorded in Hebrews 7. The writer to the Hebrews is attempting to prove that Jesus is greater than the High Priesthood of Levi or the Levitical priesthood. Levi, and the descendants of Levi, served as priests in the Temple.

To prove his point, the writer tells the story of Abraham meeting this strange character Melchizedek. Melchizedek is the priest of Salem or Jerusalem. He has no beginning nor ending. He is a priest forever and a type of Christ.

Abraham is returning from a battle with the five kings, a battle he won. He is returning with the plunder from the war and meets this strange priest of Salem. He gives to Melchizedek ten percent of the plunder indicating that Melchizedek, this type of Christ, was greater than himself since the lesser sacrifices to the greater. So, what does this have to do with Levi.

Levi was the son of Jacob, who was the son of Isaac, who was the son of Abraham. The writer says that Levi, who was "in the loins of Abraham" gave the tithe to Melchizedek indicating that Jesus was greater than Levi and the Levitical priesthood. What an interesting way of thinking. The Greek word translated "loins" is *osphys* which means the reproductive part of the human body.

So, when Adam sinned, you and I, were in the "loins of Adam," and became sinners. What happened in the past, affects us today.

The clearest demonstration of the reality of original sin or of the corrupted human nature is death. Paul writes in Romans 6:23: "For the wages of sin is death," and in 1 Corinthians 15:22: "For as in Adam all die."

At a funeral service, where perhaps friends and family stand up and speak of the goodness of the deceased, there is one fact that cannot be denied. Regardless of how many good works could be affirmed, the one who died was a sinner because the "wages of sin is death," and "death came to all men, because all sinned."

Sinners by Experience

When we were born into this world, not only were we born "in Adam" or out of the root of Adam, but the rebellious nature of Adam was born in us. We became sinners by experience. The full content of Adam's perverted nature was joined and cemented to us. Sin became our experience. Therefore, we are sinners "objectively" because we were born out of the root of Adam, and we are sinners "subjectively" because the old nature of Adam is joined to us. Our identity or position is that of being a sinner. Our life and experience are also that of being a sinner. (It is important to keep in mind this distinction between "objective" and "subjective" because it will come up again.)

The Bible is very clear in its estimate of human life. We are the children of wrath (Ephesians 2:3), totally unable by nature to grasp the things of the Spirit of God (1 Corinthians 2:14). The Bible tells us that we were shaped in iniquity and born in sin (Psalm 51:5) and that the imaginations of our hearts are evil (Genesis 8:21). Within our human flesh, there dwells no good thing.

This truth is certainly not hard to demonstrate. If you keep your eye on any little "innocent" baby that is born into this world, you will discover that the "sweet little thing" turns into a selfish, disobedient, "monster" at about the age of two or three.

At a baptism, when the truth of original sin is expounded, identifying the infant as one who is born in sin and needs the grace of God, perhaps Mom and Dad are thinking to themselves, "This might apply to other babies, but not to our sweet, innocent infant." But when the child reaches the so-called "terrible twos," Mom and Dad might be tempted to bring the child back for re-baptism, claiming it didn't work the first time.

Because we have been born in Adam, we have sinned and fallen short of the glory of God. We have not done the things God has commanded us to do, nor have we avoided the things He has commanded us not to do. Even though we seek to live moral, responsible lives and may do a fairly good job of it, our hearts are wrong. Our attitudes do not reflect the love, joy and peace which God desires for us. Our intentions and motives are primarily self-centered. Because of our pride, we are quick to break relationships and hold back forgiveness from others. Because our lives are wrapped up in ourselves, we worry about our future and fear sickness, tragedy or death. We feel sorry for ourselves. To make ourselves look good in the eyes of others, we readily judge those who do not live-up to our standards. If we do not get our way, we become angry and resentful. Putting it very simply, our lives are a mess!

If we are not happy with ourselves and set out on a pathway of self-improvement, we soon discover that the good that we want to do, we are unable to do and fall back into old habits and practices.

Step 1: I Am a Sinner Because I Sin

One time I asked a group of people in a Bible Class, "How many of you would like to be more patient, kinder, more loving, and have greater joy and peace?" Every hand went up. I responded, "Well, do it." Everyone laughed as if to say, "If we could, we would."

This is the human dilemma. The Apostle Paul clearly defined that dilemma in Romans 7. He wrote:

I do not understand what I do. For what I want to do I do not do, but what I hate I do. And if I do what I do not want to do, I agree that the law is good. As it is, it is no longer I myself who do it, but it is sin living in me. I know that nothing good lives in me, that is, in my sinful nature. For I have the desire to do what is good, but I cannot carry it out. For what I do is not the good I want to do; no, the evil I do not want to do--this I keep on doing. Now if I do what I do not want to do, it is no longer I who do it, but it is sin living in me that does it. So, I find this law at work: When I want to do good, evil is right there with me. For in my inner being I delight in God's law; but I see another law at work in the members of my body, waging war against the law of my mind and making me a prisoner of the law of sin at work within my members. What a wretched man I am!

Civil Righteousness

Some of you may respond by saying, "There are many good people in this world who are kind, considerate, do many good works by helping the less fortunate. They are intelligent, hard-working and honest but are not Christians. How can you say that human nature has been totally corrupted?"

This is true. There is a righteousness of reason or a civil righteousness. Regarding this, Philip Melanchthon, a co-worker with Martin Luther in defining the theology of the Reformation wrote in what is called the A*pology* (or defense) *of the Augsburg Confession:*

> *For God wants this civil discipline to restrain the unspiritual, and to preserve it he has given laws, learning, teaching, governments and penalties. To some extent, reason can produce this righteousness by its own strength, though it is often overwhelmed by its natural weakness and by the devil, who drives it to open crimes. We freely give this righteousness of reason its due credit; for our corrupt nature has no greater good than this.... God even honors it with material rewards.[4]*

---

[4] Tappert, *The Book of Concord,* p. 110:22

The fact is, you can refine, discipline, and educate a sinner and what you have is a refined, disciplined and educated sinner. No matter what you do, you cannot change human nature. I might discipline my dog to walk on his hind legs, dress him up in a suit and tie, but I still have a dog. In case my dog produces off-spring, they will walk on four legs and bark. Moral, responsible, disciplined parents do not give birth to moral, responsible, disciplined children.

Over the past generation there have been many who have contributed a great deal to the betterment of our society, but there is one thing they all have in common – they're dead! Because the wages of sin is death.

~~~~~

Questions for Discussion:

1. What is the result of applying the law to the sinful nature? Will putting up a sign "Don't step on the grass" keep the neighborhood kids off the grass?

2. What if you add the fear of punishment to the law? Does your driving on the highway change when you have a police car behind you? What happens when the police car

leaves the highway? Has the law changed your heart?

3. The Apostle Paul writes in Romans 3:21: "For if a law had been given that could impart life, then righteousness would certainly have come by the law." What does he mean by that?

Step 2:
Stop Playing the Blame Game

One of the poignant scenes in the movie *Good Will Hunting* is when Sean, the psychologist, the character played by the late Robin Williams, confronts Will, the oft obnoxious character played by Matt Damon, by repeatedly saying, "It's not your fault. It's not your fault. It's not your fault." Finally, there's a breakthrough in the counseling session, and the two share a tearful embrace.

We really don't know what blame Will Hunting was bearing, but perhaps it really was his fault.

It's Not My Fault!

The hardest words for a person to say are, "It's my fault." We will do anything to get out from under the heavy hand of guilt and blame other people or circumstances for our misdeeds, when in fact, we know that it is our fault.

If you live in a family with more than one child, determining which child is responsible for a misdeed is often impossible. Every child blames one of their siblings. There are times when parents are convinced that things get broken, food gets eaten, rooms get messed and walls get dirtied and no one is responsible. As the disgraced comedian Bill Cosby once

25

quipped, "Having one child is easy. If something gets broken, you know who did it."

Passing the buck and blaming other people or circumstances for our failures and mistakes is not only reserved for children. I used to play golf with a man who never did anything wrong. He always had an explanation for every errant tee shot or missed putt. It was never his fault. One day he mentioned to us that his son had been expelled from college over possession of drugs, but, of course, as he explained, it really wasn't his fault.

We never outgrow the need to justify our actions, pass the buck and blame other people or circumstances for our failures so that we will appear to be in the right. While we are very quick to pass judgment upon the actions of others, if a judgment is leveled against us, we will seek ways and means and devise various schemes to defend ourselves, even though in our hearts we know we were wrong. I am sure that all of you have been in situations in which you have contrived some rather far-fetched explanations to defend your questionable behavior.

While every Christian is theoretically willing to say, "I am a sinner, and I have fallen short of God's glory," but when "push comes to shove" over placing blame for specific incidents of sin, the same self-confessed sinner will try every means possible to avoid having the finger of accusation pointed at him.

Another "Blessing" from Adam

Why is it that we refuse to accept blame and "pass the buck" to others? To answer the question, we must go back again to Adam. Not only did we receive a sinful nature from Adam, we have also been "blessed" with other human characteristics.

In Genesis 3, after Adam and Eve had given into temptation and fallen into sin, their guilt drove them into hiding. They knew their condition. They knew they had disobeyed God but look what happens when God levels the finger of accusation.

"It's not my fault," cries Adam, "it was that woman you gave me."

"It's not my fault," Eve protests, "it was that snake you created and left roaming around the garden."

While they both knew very well they had sinned and disobeyed God, they were unwilling to accept the blame. In fact, in their eyes, God was the one who was ultimately responsible for their sin. This attitude of Adam and Eve is clearly seen in us! It is a part of human nature.

Dr. Paul Tournier wrote in his book *Guilt and Grace,*

Step 2: The Blame Game

> *In a healthy person...this defense mechanism has the precision and universality of a law of nature... We defend ourselves against criticism with the same energy we employ in defending ourselves against hunger, cold or wild beasts, for it is a mortal threat.*[5]

I have known people who are never happy, and it's never their fault. They go from marriage to marriage, or from job to job, or from one church to another church and always find something wrong. There are people who make them angry or get them upset. You would think that eventually they would conclude that there is one non-variable. Everywhere they go and in everything they do, they take one person along – themselves. Might they eventually arrive at the conclusion that perhaps they are the problem? As the comic strip character *Pogo* put it, "We have met the enemy, and he is us."

It is very hard to admit that you are the problem. For the first ten years in the ministry there were times I was very unhappy, especially when there were people in the congregations I served who were critical of me, but of course, it wasn't my fault. They were the ones who were making me miserable and discontented.

---

[5] Paul Tournier, *Guilt and Grace*, (New York: Harper and Row, 1959), p. 81.

No One to Blame

One cold November night I caught a glimpse of myself that scared the life out of me, and I had no one to blame. Just a few weeks before, my wife had come home from the hospital with our third child, a beautiful brown-eyed baby girl whom we named Susan. As is often the case with babies, and Susan was no exception, a middle of the night feeding was required.

In the midst of a deep sleep, I heard the voice of my wife, "Come on, wake-up! You feed her tonight. I'm tired."

"You gotta be kidding," I responded." In the background I could hear Susan wailing in the next room. "Can't you feed her? I'm tired too."

"I have been up with her every night since we came home," my wife responded somewhat angrily. "You can get up with her one night."

She was right. I had not yet participated in Susan's middle of the night ritual. So, I crawled out from under the warm covers.

"Brrr, it's cold..." I quietly exclaimed as my feet hit the floor. November in central Michigan is not characterized by warm nights. The clock told me it was two-fifteen. I stumbled into the next room and gently picked up my little girl out of her crib and together we headed for the kitchen. As the bottle was being warmed, she continued to wail despite my words of assurance that the bottle would soon be ready.

Step 2: The Blame Game

Finally, daddy and his little girl sat down together on the living room sofa and the feeding began. It was a beautiful cold, crisp night. The moonlight streaming in through the open drapes created an eerie effect. There was something nice about the moment, something nostalgic.

After the bottle had been sucked dry, we began walking the floor together, seeking that all-important burp. Finally, it came. Praising Susan for the fact that she worked so well, I gently lowered her from my shoulder into my arms. We paced the floor together. While I was gently singing "Jesus loves me this I know," her eyelids grew heavy, and she went back to sleep. I was proud of my accomplishment. I was eagerly anticipating jumping back under the warm covers with a sense of satisfaction over a job well done.

Tip-toeing back down the hallway to her room, I very carefully lowered her into her crib and covered her with a blanket. She looked so beautiful, so much at peace. Gently closing her door behind me, I headed back to bed. Just as I had pulled the warm covers around me, closed my eyes and began to drift off...., I heard the worst possible sound. Susan began to scream...

I discovered an intense anger and rage welling-up within me. I quickly jumped out of bed and angrily marched down the hall to

Susan's room. Just as I pushed open the door, the thought crossed my mind: "See what kind of a person you are..." I stopped dead in my tracks. My anger subsided.

"Wow," I thought to myself as I gently lifted Susan from the crib, "I could have struck my little girl." I felt so very ashamed and even apologized to my baby for my anger. As far as I was concerned, any person who would strike a helpless infant is the ultimate low-life. Yet, I was capable of doing such a thing. I had been on the brink of losing control, gripped by an anger and rage over the fact that my little daughter was taking away my comfort, robbing me of a few extra moments of sleep. How could I blame her for getting me so angry? It was my fault.

After numerous other less dramatic experiences, I concluded that given the right set of circumstances, I was capable of anything. I was convinced that there was no sin that I could not commit, no perverse act in which I could not participate if the conditions were right. For the very first time in my life, I saw myself as God saw me: wretched, pitiful, poor, blind and naked, and I had no one to blame. It was my fault.

I was forced to change my way of thinking. No one had the power to make me angry or get me upset. My little baby didn't get me angry. How could I blame her? Rather, I got myself angry. I got myself bent out of shape and upset over the things people may say or do. It was my fault. I met the enemy, and it was me. I didn't have a host of problems identified by circumstances and the attitudes and actions of other people. I had one problem, and it was me. No longer did I pray that God would change my circumstances so that I might be happy. Rather, God, change me!

The Gospel

I threw myself into a renewed study of the Gospel of Jesus Christ: the forgiveness of sins and the truth of justification by grace through faith. It was only after the Apostle Paul had established the stark reality and consequences of human sin in the Book of Romans did he present the Good News of the forgiveness of sins and justification by grace. The Gospel of Jesus Christ became a life-changing message of Divine grace.

The seventeenth century philosopher and theologian Blaise Pascal wrote:

For if we could face ourselves, with all our faults, we would then be so shaken out of complacency, triviality, indifference, and pretense that a deep longing for strength and truth would be aroused within us. Not until man is aware of his deepest need is he ready to discern and grasp what can meet his deepest need.[6]

Martin Luther wrote:

"The righteous man is one who accuses himself first" Therefore "even if he falls seven times a day, he as often rises again" in that he does not excuse himself for his sins, but quickly confesses them and accuses himself. With that his sins are at once forgiven him, and he has risen again. This is evident in the case of David in 2 Sam. 12:13. As soon as he had said, "I have sinned," Nathan answered, "the Lord has taken your sin away...." On the contrary, those who set up their own righteousness and excuse themselves for their sins (like Saul, like Adam and Eve) do not judge themselves or accuse themselves but think they are doing well and are pleased with themselves and love themselves and their own life in this world.[7]

There is a reciprocal relationship between sin and grace, the acknowledgment of fault and the appreciation for forgiveness. In observing

---

[6] David E. Roberts, *Existentialism and Religious Belief,* (New York: Oxford University Press, 1959) p. 99.

[7] Martin Luther, *Luther's Works,* (Saint Louis: Concordia Publishing House, 1974) Vol. 10: Psalms 1-75.

this reality in his patients, Dr. Paul Tournier writes:

> *This can be seen in history; for believers who are the most desperate about themselves are the ones who express most forcefully their confidence in grace...Those who are the most pessimistic about man are the most optimistic about God; those who are the most severe with themselves are the ones who have the most serene confidence in divine forgiveness... By degrees the awareness of our guilt and of God's love increase side by side.* [8]

When you consider the human condition, you might very well respond by saying, "This is not fair. Every person born into this world is doomed to begin with. They have no choice in the matter, and as far as God is concerned, it's their own fault."

The Apostle Paul writes in Romans 11:32: "For God has bound everyone over to disobedience so that he may have mercy on them all." God's purpose from the very beginning was to show his great love to the world of sinners by offering the forgiveness of sins and eternal life. For God so loved this world of sinners that he sent His only Son so that whoever believes in him will not perish but

---

[8] Paul Tournier, *Guilt and Grace*, pp. 159-160.

have eternal life (John 3:16). We read in 1 Timothy 2:4 that God "wants all people to be saved and to come to a knowledge of the truth."

Do you see yourself as God sees you – a sinner in need of His grace? Are you willing to embrace the reality of your sinful nature and accuse yourself rather than passing the blame to other people? If so, I have some very good news for you.

~~~~

Questions for Discussion:

1. Why is it so hard for you to say, "It's my fault?"

2. If you apologetically go to a person with whom you have had a conflict and say, "I'm sorry. It was my fault," how does that person usually respond?

3. Obviously, not everything is your fault. There are circumstances beyond your control. But, are you responsible for how you respond to those circumstances? If your response is anger, resentment, and bitterness, it is your fault?

Step 3:
Sins are Forgiven because Jesus'
BLOOD
was Shed on the Cross.
(For no other reason!)

Why should God forgive your sins?

If you would ask a Christian that question, I am quite sure that many would answer, "Because God loves me."

There is truth to that answer. The Bible says that God so loved the world that He gave his only Son (John 3:16). While love is what motivated God to forgive the sins of the world, love is not the cause or the reason why God forgives. God forgives because His justice has been satisfied.

Consider the relationship between love and justice.

Let's say a judge, seated on the bench, is asked to sentence a young man who was convicted of committing a crime and deserved to be punished, and that *young man happened to be his son.* Would love and justice be in conflict? While the love of the father for his son would not want to see him punished; the judge, who is just, would be forced to impose the punishment. Justice would have to be satisfied.

Atonement

Sin is an atrocity in the eyes of God. The Apostle Paul writes in Romans 1:18: "The wrath of God is being revealed from heaven against all the godlessness and wickedness of people, who suppress the truth by their wickedness." In the Old Testament there are numerous references to the wrath of God against his disobedient people. The Psalmist writes (6:1), O Lord, do not rebuke me in your anger or discipline me in your wrath."

Within the biblical context, the word "atonement" means to appease or to set aside the wrath of God. Atonement for sin requires the shedding of blood. Leviticus 17:11 says, "For the life of a creature is in the blood, and I have given it to you to make atonement for yourselves on the altar; it is the blood that makes atonement for one's life." We read in Hebrew 9:22: "Without the shedding of blood there is no forgiveness."

I'm sure that such references are offensive to the sensibilities of some folk. God seems to be described as a "blood-thirsty" God and not the sweet, kind deity we might prefer. But think about it. If God had imposed some lesser requirement for atonement to take place it would not be an accurate depiction of the attributes of God. The severe requirements for atonement underlines the utter holiness and justice of God and His disdain for sin. God takes your sin very seriously.

In the Old Testament, alongside the requirements of the Law, God established the sacrificial system whereby sins could be forgiven and atonement, or the setting aside of the wrath of God, could take place. There had to exist among the faithful Israelites, especially among the children, a sensitivity to sin since it required the sacrifice of an innocent animals over and over again. Imagine...

Why Does the Lamb Have to Die?

It is the morning of the Sabbath and the family of Isaak and Miriam and their two children, Jonathan and Rachel are preparing to go to the Tabernacle.

"Jonathan, go out to the sheepfold and get a lamb," Isaak instructs his son.

This is a weekly chore that Jonathan hated since he knew many of the lambs by name and some of them he regarded as his pets, but it had to be done. He picks up one of the lambs and hands it to his father.

On their way to the Tabernacle, Jonathan asks his father,

"Dad, why does this lamb have to die?"

"Well, Jonathan," his Father replied. "Think of the many things this week that you and your sister did that were wrong. You often disobeyed your Mom and me when you knew it was wrong and a sin against God. There were times when your Mother and I got into arguments with each other and got angry. We have all done things that were wrong and sins against God. For this reason, the lamb has to die."

Upon arriving at the Tabernacle, the family is met by one of the priests who takes the lamb from Isaak. Isaak lays his hands upon the lamb imparting the sins of his family to the lamb. The priest slits the throat of the lamb, gathers the blood in a basin and sprinkles it upon the altar. The lamb is then offered up as a burnt offering for the sins of the family.

On the way back home, Jonathan asks his Father,

"Can we be sure that God has forgiven our sins?"

"Yes, Jonathan," Isaak replied. "We can be sure, because the lamb died."

When John the Baptist saw Jesus coming toward him he said, "'Look, the Lamb of God, who takes away the sin of the world!" (John 1:29) I'm sure most of the people were puzzled by John's statement. John predicted that Jesus would be the lamb sacrificed for the sins of the world.

This sacrifice of Jesus on the cross would be once and for all, unlike the sacrifices in the Old Testament.

Consider these verses from the New Testament regarding the sacrifice of Jesus on the cross and the shedding of His blood for our atonement and redemption. The word "redemption" means to buy back or to ransom. The blood of Jesus Christ redeemed us from sin, death and the power of the devil. In his explanation of the Second Article of the Apostles' Creed, Martin Luther writes concerning Jesus: "Who has redeemed me, a lost and condemned person, purchased and won me from all sins, from death, and from the power of the devil; not with gold or silver, but with His holy, precious blood and with His innocent suffering and death."

Romans 3:25: "God presented him as a sacrifice of atonement, through faith in his blood."

Ephesians 1:7-8: "In him we have redemption through his blood, the forgiveness of sins, in accordance with the riches of God's grace that he lavished on us with all wisdom and understanding."

Hebrews 9:13-14,22: "The blood of goats and bulls and the ashes of a heifer sprinkled on those who are ceremonially unclean sanctify them so that they are outwardly clean. How much more, then, will the blood of Christ, who through the eternal Spirit offered himself unblemished to God, cleanse our consciences from acts that lead to death, so that we may serve the living God! In fact, the law requires that nearly everything be cleansed with blood, and without the shedding of blood there is no forgiveness."

This sacrifice of Jesus on the cross would be once and for all, unlike the sacrifices in the Old Testament. The writer to the Hebrews declares:

"He did not enter by means of the blood of goats and calves; but he entered the Most Holy Place once for all by his own blood, having obtained eternal redemption. (9:12)"

A "Covenant Thing"

When Jesus, on the night before He was crucified, gathered with his disciples and gave to them and to all Christians the Lord's Supper, he passed the cup to His disciples and said, "This is my blood of the covenant, which is poured out for many." (Mark 14:24) The shed blood of Jesus on the cross is a "covenant thing." It is an agreement between God and man. In the Old Testament, if the lamb died, sins were forgiven. In the same way, through the New Covenant, through the shedding of the blood of Jesus, sins are forgiven.

In the Book of Exodus, we read the account of the Passover. The final plague visited upon the Egyptians was the death of the first-born son of each household. The Jews were instructed to take some of the blood of the Passover lamb and apply it to the doorposts of their houses. God said to Moses, "The blood will be a sign for you on the houses where you are; and when I see the blood, I will pass over you." (Exodus 12:13) God did not say, "I may pass over you," or "If you're lucky, I might pass over you." No, it was a "covenant thing." If God saw the blood, there is no doubt that no harm would befall the people who lived in that house.

The shed blood of Jesus on the cross is a covenant between God and man. Because the blood of Jesus was shed, God forgives sins. For this reason, Martin Luther wrote,

> *When Satan instills the notion into me that God is not gracious to me, that idea is a sin of blasphemy, for God has commanded us to expect the forgiveness of sins from this Christ. He therefore who does not do so turns God into a liar.* [9]

The forgiveness of sins is objective. If you recall from the First Step, we became sinners objectively when Adam sinned. In the same way, the forgiveness of sins took place outside of us, two-thousand years ago when Jesus shed His blood on the cross. This forgiveness applies to the entire world of sinners. John writes in 1 John 2:2: "He is the atoning sacrifice for our sins, but not only for ours, but also for the sins of the whole world."

When we share our faith with others, we do not say, "When you become a Christian your sins will be forgiven." Rather we declare, "Jesus died for you and shed His blood for you. Your sins are forgiven." This is the Gospel we

---

[9] Plass, *What Luther Says, p. 519*

proclaim. This does not mean that every person is going to heaven because God has forgiven the sins of the entire world. This is the position of Universalism. Rather, when the Holy Spirit bring a person to faith through the preaching of the Gospel, they receive the benefits of their forgiveness, namely, deliverance from sin, death and the power of the devil and eternal life in heaven.

How Do You Know?

As I shared in the Introduction, every Christian Church believes that the forgiveness of sins is central. For this reason, church groups display a cross in the front of their sanctuaries. The differences are in what comes before and after the cross.

One of the major distortions is taught by the Reformed Church or those groups who follow the teachings of John Calvin. Calvin taught a "limited atonement." Jesus died on the cross to forgive the sins of those who are the elect. Election, or what is called predestination, comes before the cross. Those who hold to this view cannot declare to a person, "Jesus died for you. Your sins are forgiven" because they don't know whether or not that person is a part of the elect. In answer to the question, "How do you know your sins are forgiven?' the Calvinist would answer, "Because I am a part of the elect," to which one might respond, "Are you sure?"

Some would say, "I know my sins are forgiven because I made a decision, went forward and got saved." This is called "decision theology" and was introduced into the church in the middle of the nineteenth century through the work of the evangelist Charles Finney.

A teenage girl in one of my congregations attended a Baptist summer camp. Evenings, seated around the campfire, one of the songs they sang was "Name the Day When You were Saved" and the group would point at an individual who would name the day when he or she went forward and got saved.

In speaking with her before she went off to camp, she was concerned.

"I know that they're going to point at me, and I won't know what to say."

"Tell them Friday," I responded. "Good Friday when Jesus shed His blood on the cross."

For several years, I did Christian talk radio. On a Good Friday I interviewed an author who had written what I thought was a decent book on the Cross. With only a few minutes left in the program, I asked the question,

"If there are those listening to us today who are not sure that their sins are forgiven, what would you tell them?"

"Well," he answered. "I would want to know if they had repented of all known sins."

"Uh oh," I thought. "I have a problem."

I said good-bye to my guest and thanked him for the interview. After disconnecting the phone line, I had about forty-five seconds to clean up the mess.

"Listen folks," I began. "If you aren't sure your sins are forgiven, it's not about repenting of all known sins but asking yourself the simple question: 'Did Jesus shed His blood on the cross or didn't He? If He did, your sins are forgiven."

I had a man tell me that he knew his sins were forgiven because he had prayed the "sinner's prayer" and was really sorry for his sins.

"Are you sure you were really sincere and sorry enough?" I asked.

"I hope so," he responded.

You are not forgiven because you're sorry for your sins. You are forgiven because the blood of Christ was shed for you.

Because of a distortion in preaching, there are people within my own Lutheran Church who would erroneously answer the question by saying, "I know my sins are forgiven because I've been baptized." It is much easier for lazy preachers to assure people of their salvation by telling them "Have no fear. You have been baptized," rather than having to expound the message of the Gospel.

Baptism, particularly infant Baptism, is a part of the "delivery system" whereby the benefits of the suffering and death of Jesus are delivered. It would be accurate to say, "I know my sins are forgiven because the blood of Christ was shed on the cross, and I know I have the benefits of His shed blood because I have been baptized." Sometime Christians are encouraged to "remember their Baptism." This is good, but I would prefer to have Christians encouraged to remember that the Lord Jesus shed His blood on the Cross for them.

Finally, there are those who might say, "I know my sins are forgiven because I confessed my sins and received absolution or forgiveness from the Pastor. Confession and Absolution are an integral part of the worship life of the church. It provides a means whereby we "tap into" the great benefits of the suffering and death of our Lord Jesus, something Christians need to do every day.

The forgiveness of sins is not about you and what you have done or experienced. Your sins are forgiven because Jesus suffered and died on the cross and shed His blood for you. Case closed!

~~~~

Questions for Discussion:

1. How is it possible that the suffering and death of Jesus on the Cross was sufficient to tip the scales of divine justice and provide forgiveness for the sins of the entire world, past, present and future?

2. In Galatians 6:7, the Apostle Paul writes: "Do not be deceived: God cannot be mocked. A man reaps what he sows." Does the forgiveness of sins remove temporal consequences?

3. On a human level, we may claim to forgive but not forget. Jeremiah 31:34 says, "I will forgive their wickedness and will remember their sins no more." How is it possible for God who is all knowing to forget our sins against Him?

Step 4:
Faith Receives the Promises of God.
Faith is the Hand that Reaches Out
and Grasps the Promise.

There is a great deal of confusion in the minds of Christians when it comes to the subject of faith. I have heard people referred to as "great men or women of faith." The term "faith based" is applied to religious institutions or organizations. Faith implies being certain of something even where there is no evidence or proof. The Bible says we are "saved by grace through faith." (Ephesians 2:8) What is this thing called "faith?" In the New Testament, the same Greek word or derivative of is used for both "faith" and "believe"

General Faith

There is a "general faith in God." In the minds of some, a Christian is one who believes in God. There is no scientific proof for the existence of God, but it is both reasonable and logical to conclude that such a Being exists. The Greek philosopher Aristotle observed that all things were in motion and concluded that there must be an "unmoved mover," someone who set things in motion. There are numerous arguments designed to prove the existence of God.

The Bible never sets out to prove the existence of God but assumes it to be true. The Bible begins, "In the beginning, God...." The Apostle Paul writes in Romans 1:18-20:

Step 4: Faith Receives the Promises of God.

The wrath of God is being revealed from heaven against all the godlessness and wickedness of men who suppress the truth by their wickedness, since what may be known about God is plain to them, because God has made it plain to them. For since the creation of the world God's invisible qualities--his eternal power and divine nature--have been clearly seen, being understood from what has been made, so that men are without excuse.

It is not a profound expression of religious fervor for a person to confess to believe in God. James writes: "You believe that there is one God. Good! Even the demons believe that--and shudder." (2:9) A general faith or belief in God is not what the Bible speaks of as "saving faith." The motto of the United States is "In God We Trust." While we purport to be a God-fearing nation, this does not identify us as being a Christian nation.

Faith or Facts?

"Historical faith" believes that the events recorded in Scripture, specifically the New Testament events about the life of Jesus, are true. Some erroneously identify themselves as Christians because they believe by faith that the events of the birth, life, death, resurrection and ascension of Jesus are true.

When I was doing talk-radio I interviewed an archaeologist who spoke of the recent discoveries confirming the truth of Scripture concerning Jesus. One lady called into the program and said, "I don't need archaeology. I have faith." For her, being a Christian meant accepting by faith the historical events in the life of Jesus and the factual evidence of archaeology was a threat to her "blind faith."

Do we accept the events in the life of Jesus recorded in the Gospel by faith or are they facts of history?

We believe many historical events of the past even though there are no longer any eye-witnesses to confirm that those events occurred. I believe, for example, the Revolutionary War happened, even though there are no living eye-witnesses. I can read eye-witness testimony and travel to Lexington, Concord or Boston and view the sites where the great battles were fought.

Why is it any different when we deal with the documents recording the events in the life of Jesus? The Gospel writer Luke described his method of research in presenting the life of Jesus.

Many have undertaken to draw up an account of the things that have been

Step 4: Faith Receives the Promises of God.

fulfilled among us, just as they were handed down to us by those who from the first were eyewitnesses and servants of the word. Therefore, since I myself have carefully investigated everything from the beginning, it seemed good also to me to write an orderly account for you, most excellent Theophilus, so that you may know the certainty of the things you have been taught. (1:1-4)

Since Luke provided eye-witness testimony, and I can travel to Israel and view the sites where those recorded events took place, I don't accept the truth of the events in the life of Jesus by faith no more than I accept the event of the Revolutionary War by faith. I accept those events as facts of history.

You may disagree and argue that the events describing the Revolutionary War depict natural events whereas the Gospel writer depict supernatural events, such as the miracles of Jesus and His resurrection from the dead. Such events are contrary to reason and hard to believe and must be accepted by faith.

In addition to claiming that Luke and the other Gospel writers were purposely lying and making up stories about miracles, there is evidence that such miracles took place as reported. In the Gospel of Mark, there is an

Step 4: Faith Receives the Promises of God.

intriguing account of Jesus healing a blind man in a two-step process:

> *And He came to Bethsaida. And they brought a blind man to Him and begged Him to touch him. And He took the blind man by the hand and led him out of the town. And when He had spat on his eyes and had put His hands on him, He asked Him if he saw anything. And he looked up and said, I see men as trees, walking. And after that He put His hands again on his eyes and made him look up. And he was restored and saw all clearly' (Mark 8:22-25).*

In his book *An Anthropologist on Mars*[10] Oliver Sacks, Professor of Neurology at the Albert Einstein College of Medicine, New York, tells the story of Virgil, a 50-year-old man, blind from childhood, whose sight was restored in 1991 after a cataract was removed and a new lens implanted in one eye.

When the bandages were removed, Virgil could see, but he had no idea what he was seeing. His brain could make no sense of the images that his optic nerve was transmitting. Although he now had eyesight, he was still mentally blind, a condition known medically as

---

[10] Sacks, O., *An Anthropologist on Mars*, (Knoff, A.A., New York, 1995), pp. 108-152.

agnosia, the inability of the brain to recognize sensory input. A cat was particularly puzzling, as he could see parts clearly, a paw, the nose, the tail, but the cat as a whole was only a blur. Virgil said that 'trees didn't look like anything on earth', but a month later he finally put a tree together and realized that the trunk and leaves formed a complete unit. This true story was made into a film *At First Sight*, released in 1999, starring Val Kilmer as Virgil.

In his *Breakpoint* newsletter, the late Charles Colson compared Virgil to the man who said to Jesus, "I see men as trees walking,"

> *As Keith Mano writes in the <u>National Review</u>, this phrase "is not a poetic image. It is a clinical description. Like Virgil, the Bethsaida man can now see, but he cannot yet make sense of what he is seeing. Tree and man run together, as did trunk and tree-top for Virgil." In short, Mano concludes, "this is irrefutable evidence that a miracle did occur at Bethsaida No [charlatan] in the crowd could have faked it all by pretending to be blind because only someone recently given his sight would see 'men as trees, walking'.... A faker, not knowing about post-blind syndrome, would have reported that Jesus had given him perfect vision." Instead, the Gospel reports that Jesus*

Step 4: Faith Receives the Promises of God.

cured the man twice: once of blindness and then of post-blind syndrome. In the age of science, skeptics and even some Christians are all too eager to explain away the miracles of Christ. They claim that advances in science will eventually provide a naturalistic explanation for what appear to be supernatural events. But ironically, as Virgil's story shows, science is providing a wonderful apologetic for Christianity. The story of the blind man's miraculous healing by Jesus could not be fully understood until our own day, when modern medicine has revealed the true nature of blindness.[11]

Medical science has "caught up" to Jesus. If this one miracle is obviously true, why not all of them?

Regarding the Resurrection of Jesus from the dead, the central event in Christianity, noted apologist John Warwick Montgomery, who is both a theologian and a lawyer, claims that he could prove to a jury beyond a reasonable doubt that Jesus was raised from the dead.

Simon Greenleaf, the founder of Harvard Law School, was an atheist and agnostic. He was challenged by one of his students to

---

[11] Charles Colson, *Breakpoint*, February 11, 1999

disprove the Resurrection of Jesus. In his famous essay, *Testimony of the Evangelists Examined by the Rules of Evidence Administered in Courts of Justice,* he arrived at the conclusion that the Resurrection of Jesus was factual. As a result, he became a Christian

In addition to the biblical record, extra-biblical material from the Jewish historian Josephus, the Roman historian Tacitus, the pagan Mara Bar Serapion and others confirm the fact that Jesus was crucified under Pontius Pilate, buried in Jerusalem, and the message of the Resurrection was first preached in Jerusalem.

That being the case, there is no doubt that the tomb was empty since the Resurrection could not be proclaimed in Jerusalem if the dead body of Jesus was still in the tomb. While there are theories as to why the tomb was empty, none of them are logically tenable. The only reasonable conclusion is that Jesus was raised from the dead.

In Acts 26, the Apostle Paul is making his defense before King Agrippa and declares that it was necessary that the Messiah should suffer and die and be raised from the dead. The Governor Festus accuses Paul of being insane. Paul responds, "'I am not insane, most excellent Festus, what I am saying is true and reasonable. The king is familiar with these things, and I can speak freely to him. I am convinced that none of this has escaped his notice, because it was not done in a corner.'"

To ignore all evidence and piously claim to have an "historical faith" does not identify one as a Christian and is certainly not a "saving faith."

What is Saving Faith?

When the Apostle Paul wrote in Ephesians 2:8-9: "For it is by grace you have been saved, through faith, and this not from yourselves, it is the gift of God, not by works, so that no one can boast," what did he mean by "faith?"

"Saving faith" is not directed at the events of the death and resurrection of Jesus but at the *benefits* received from those events. It is one thing to say, "I believe Jesus died and rose again." It is something quite different to say that *because* Jesus died and rose again my sins are forgiven and I have eternal life in heaven.

Regarding faith, the *Augsburg Confession* states:

> *Hence there was very great need to treat of and to restore this teaching concerning faith in Christ in order that anxious consciences should not be deprived of consolation but know that grace and forgiveness of sins are apprehended by faith in Christ. Men are also admonished that here the term "faith" does not signify mere knowledge of the*

Step 4: Faith Receives the Promises of God.

> *history (such as is in the ungodly and the devil), but it signifies faith which believes not only the history but also the effect of the history, namely, this article of the forgiveness of sins — that is, that we have grace, righteousness, and forgiveness of sins through Christ.*[12]

Faith is not some non-descript emotion about God or the mere acknowledgment of historical events. Faith is very specific. Faith grasps the promises of God. Where you have a promise, such as the promise of the forgiveness of sin, faith is active. It is the hand that reaches out and grasps the promise. Various words such as claim, apprehend, appropriate are used to define this action of faith.

In 2 Corinthians 1:20, the Apostle Paul writes: "For no matter how many promises God has made, they are "Yes" in Christ. And so, through him the "Amen" is spoken by us to the glory of God." God has promised to forgive our sins. That promised is affirmed in the sacrificial death of Jesus on the cross, and what is our response? We declare "Amen," and affirm by faith that the promise belongs to us.

But on the other hand, claiming to have faith where there is no promise is presumption. There are preachers today who proclaim a "prosperity gospel," claiming that it is the will of

---

[12] Tappert, *The Book of Concord*, p. 2, XX, 22-23

God for every believer to prosper in this world, but no such promise exists. It is not a good thing to presume upon God.

To understand the nature of faith, think of three words: knowledge, agreement and trust.

You cannot believe in Jesus and claim the forgiveness of sins unless you know that Jesus died on the cross and shed his blood for your salvation. The Apostle Paul writes in Romans 10:14: "How, then, can they call on the one they have not believed in? And how can they believe in the one of whom they have not heard? And how can they hear without someone preaching to them?" The starting point for faith is the knowledge of the truth

Perhaps from childhood you were taught the truth about Jesus and his, life, death and resurrection. You believe it and agree with it. You speak the words of the Apostles' Creed, "I believe in the forgiveness of sins."

But there is still one thing lacking: trust. The confident assurance that because Jesus died for you, *your* sins are forgiven, and you have eternal life.

Think of it in this way:

Let's say I place a parachute on a table in front of you and explain to you what it is and how it works. You have knowledge.

From there, I take you to an open field and a plane flies over and a man jumps out and his parachute opens, and he drifts to the ground, safe and sound. So, you agree that a parachute works.

Next, we board a plane and fly to five thousand feet, I put the parachute on your back, open the door and say, "Go!"

You have moved from knowledge, to agreement, to trust.

Martin Luther wrote that "hunger is the best cook." By this he meant that those who have heard the Law and judgment of God and are concerned for their eternal salvation are more ready to hear the Good News of the Gospel. For this reason, it was necessary for you to know of your lost and sinful condition and to stop blaming other people for your faults and failures. If that truth hit home, knowing that Jesus died for your forgiveness is very Good News. Or, to put it another way, if the plane happened to be on fire and was doomed to crash, you would be far more willing to strap on the parachute and jump out the door. For this reason, the preaching of the Law and the wrath of God and convicting a person of their sin is a necessary pre-condition for the preaching of the good news of the Gospel.

Faith is a Gift.

We cannot work up faith or choose to believe the benefits of the death and resurrection of Jesus. Faith is a gift and is produced by the Holy Spirit through the preaching of the Good News about Jesus. The Apostle Paul writes in Romans 10:17: "Consequently, faith comes from hearing the message, and the message is heard through the word of Christ," and in 1 Corinthians 1:21: "For since in the wisdom of God the world through its wisdom did not know him, God was pleased through the foolishness of what was preached to save those who believe."

The Bible reveals the triune or three-in-one nature of God. In general, we refer to the Father as the Creator; the Son, Jesus, as the Redeemer, and the Holy Spirit as the Sanctifier. It is the work of the Holy Spirit to create faith, and he does so through the hearing of the Gospel of Jesus Christ.

It is the responsibility of every Christian pastor to clearly preach the message of the Gospel every Sunday, allowing the Holy Spirit to create and strengthen the faith of those who hear the message.

In one of my congregations, one of my elders said to me, "Pastor, you preach the same thing every Sunday."

"I know," I responded. "Are you getting tired of hearing it."

"No!" he replied emphatically.

While there are people who sit in the pew who might complain about their pastor's preaching, I have never heard it said, "I am getting so tired of my pastor's sermons. Can you believe it! He tells me every Sunday that I am a sinner, and that God has forgiven my sins so there is no doubt that I am going to heaven. I'm sick of hearing it."

No one gets sick and tired of hearing the Gospel!

Now read this very carefully:

Because you were born out of the root of Adam, you are a sinner. As a result, you daily sin much and deserve the wrath and punishment of God. But God loves you and sent His Son Jesus into the world to bear your sins and to suffer and die on the Cross so that the justice of God has been satisfied and your sins, no matter how great or small, have been fully forgiven. You are right with God and if by chance, you should die tonight, you have eternal life with God in heaven,

Did you get it? If not, read it again.

Faith is both passive and active. Passive because it is produced by the Holy Spirit. As a result of hearing the Gospel, we are "acted upon" by the Holy Spirit.

Faith is active because once produced, it actively appropriates the promise of the forgiveness of sins and eternal life.

Faith is instrumental not causative. Your sins are not forgiven on account of your faith. Faith does not "cause" forgiveness to take place. You are not saved because you believe. Your sins are forgiven on account of the suffering and death of Jesus. Faith is instrumental. It is the hand that reaches out and receive the promise or the fork that transfers the food on your plate into your mouth.

In summary:

Your sins, together with the sins of the entire world, were objectively forgiven when Jesus suffered and died on the Cross.

The benefits of that great forgiveness are delivered to us today through the preaching of the Gospel.

Faith, passively produced in us by the Holy Spirit working through the Gospel, actively appropriates, receives, or apprehends those benefits.

Got it?

Now the question is: Because your sins are forgiven does that mean you are righteous before God? The answer is yes! The problem is, many Christian don't understand that. Let's consider the issue.

~~~~

Questions for Discussion:

1. When I mentioned to a fellow pastor that many people sitting in the pews are not sure of their salvation, he replied, "Down in their

hearts they believe in Jesus." Can a person have saving faith and not know it?

2. James writes that faith, "if it is not accompanied by action, is dead (2:17)." Does this mean that we are also saved by doing good works? Is it possible to have saving faith without doing good works?

3. A popular Bible teacher wrote a book titled, "Having Faith in Your Faith." What is wrong with that idea?

Step 5:
God does not "Grade on a Curve." The Standard is Perfection!

If you want to throw out a question that will cause some heated discussion, ask. "When you stand before God on judgment day, is it necessary that you have a perfect righteousness?"

I guarantee that most will say "No," and underline their answer by adding, "Nobody is perfect."

"No," you respond. "That is not true. There is one person who walked the face of this earth who was absolutely perfect in thought, word, and deed and his name is Jesus, and Jesus demanded the same righteousness and perfection of his disciples."

Consider the following verses:

Matthew 5:20: Jesus said: "For I tell you that unless your righteousness surpasses that of the Pharisees and the teachers of the law, you will certainly not enter the kingdom of heaven."

In response to that question, the disciples asked, "Who will ever be saved?" Jesus replied, "With man it is impossible, but with God all things are possible."

Matthew 5:48: Jesus said: "Be perfect, therefore, as your heavenly Father is perfect."

According to Jesus, the divine standard for righteousness is the very righteousness and holiness of God himself.

James 2:10: "For whoever keeps the whole law and yet stumbles at just one point is guilty of breaking all of it."

If you are hanging from a cliff by a chain made up of one hundred links and one link breaks, it is no consolation to say that ninety-nine of them didn't break.

In the *Apology of the Augsburg Confession,* Philip Melanchthon wrote that there are men who imagine that we can keep the law in such a way as to do even more than it requires, but Scripture cries out everywhere that we are far away from the perfection that the law requires.[13]

If the standard for righteousness before God is absolute perfection, how will we ever attain it? Can you imagine making a New Year's resolution, "From now on I will be perfect." Most Christians today are unwilling to even entertain such a demand or requirement.

I saw a bumper sticker that read, "Not Perfect, Just Forgiven." Obviously, the person who attached the bumper sticker had not read the words of Jesus.

God does not Grade on a Curve.

A friend of mine went to law school. She was telling me that all the professors graded on a curve, meaning your competition was not

---

[13] Tappert, *Apology of the Augsburg Confession*, I, VI, 45

against some perfect standard, but you were competing with the rest of the members of your class.

In the thinking of many, God grades humanity on a curve. We may look good when compared to other people, but God does not compare us with other people. The Divine standard for holiness is God's perfect righteousness. There are no "good Christians." Jesus said, "Be perfect!"

Good enough is not good enough. You will seldom hear the deceased at a funeral be described as a "righteous man." No, but he was a "good man." Goodness is based on that notion that God grades "on a curve." Certainly, there are people out there who are "better" than you are, but there are far more people who are "worse." So, the goal is a good, solid C+ or perhaps even a B-.

While many evangelical Christians will dismiss the notion of perfection and proclaim, "Not perfect, just forgiven," the Roman Catholic Church gets it right by recognizing that to enter the joy of heaven one must be perfectly purified. This is accomplished with the invention of purgatory. Paragraph 1030 in the *Catechism of the Catholic Church* states that all who die in God's grace and friendship, but still imperfectly purified, are indeed assured of their eternal salvation; but after death they undergo purification, to achieve the holiness necessary to enter the joy of heaven.

If you recognize the divine standard of holiness and perfection, purgatory seems to be the only alternative. It is reasonable and consistent with the human condition. If the divine standard is perfection and I evaluate my human condition, recognize my sin and failure, how will I attain the holiness necessary to enter the joy of heaven? Purgatory is a reasonable solution. That is, until one understands the Gospel.

Forgiveness and Righteousness

In the *Lutheran Confessions*, the writing, drawn from Scripture that form the basis for Lutheran theology, the forgiveness of sins and righteousness before God are connected. In Article IV of the *Augsburg Confession*, we read:

> *It is also taught among us that we cannot obtain forgiveness of sin and righteousness before God by our own merits, works, or satisfactions, but that we receive forgiveness of sin and become righteous before God by grace, for Christ's sake, through faith, when we believe that Christ suffered for us and that for his sake our sin is forgiven and righteousness and eternal life are given to us. For God will regard and*

Step 5: The Standard is Perfection.

reckon this faith as righteousness, as Paul says in Romans 3:21-26 and 4:5.[14]

In the thinking of Christians today, even Lutheran Christians, there is a disconnect between the forgiveness of sins and righteousness. If you ask a Christian "Are your sins forgiven?' they would reply in the affirmative. Every Christian knows that Jesus died on the cross to forgive the sins of the world, but the sins that they continually confess have a way of always coming back to haunt them. So, while they are forgiven, they do not regard themselves as righteous.

For this reason, they are not certain they are going to heaven when they die.

Some years ago, Dr. James D. Kennedy, the late pastor of Coral Ridge Presbyterian Church in Fort Lauderdale, designed what became a very popular evangelism program. The program consisted of asking probing questions, the first one being "if you died tonight, would you know for sure that you were going to heaven?"

With some level of fear and trembling, I decided to throw out that question to the seventy-five or so members of my Sunday morning Bible Class, asking them to raise their

---

[14] Tappert, *Augsburg Confession*, IV, 1-3

hand if they knew for sure they were going to heaven if they died tonight.

I was shocked by the response. Three people, all of them adult converts who had gone through the adult confirmation class and had been taught the relationship between forgiveness of sins and righteousness before God, raised their hands. Many of the others in the group gave them that "who do you think you are" look. They were not certain of their eternal salvation because they did not confidently believe they were righteous enough.

Martin Luther's Struggle with Sin

If there was ever a person who deeply struggled with the issue of sin and righteousness it was Martin Luther. He asked, "How could a sinful person stand confidently before a perfectly righteous and holy God." He declared that he hated the God who demanded perfect holiness from a person who was born in sin.

He knew and understood the forgiveness of sins and participated daily in "Confession and Absolution." but he was not at peace. He tried everything to become righteous before God. He joined a monastery and attempted to quiet his conscience by beating himself or wearing a "hair-shirt" (You itch so much you can't be tempted to sin.). In 1512, he visited Rome and climbed on his knees the *Scala Sancta*, "the holy stairs."[15] No matter what he did, he could find no peace.

Luther described himself as a good monk who kept his orders so strictly that he could say that if ever a monk could get to heaven through monastic discipline, he should have entered it. All his companions in the monastery who knew him would agree. For if it had gone on much longer, he would have martyred himself to death, with vigils, prayers, reading and other works. He said,

> *I tried to live according to the Rule with all diligence, and I used to be contrite, to confess and number my sins, and often repeated my confession, and sedulously performed my allotted penance. And yet my conscience could never give me certainty, but I always doubted and said, "You did not perform that correctly. You were not contrite enough. You left that out of your confession." The more I tried to remedy an uncertain, weak and afflicted conscience with the traditions of men, the more each*

---

[15] According to Roman Catholic tradition, the Holy Stairs are the steps leading up to the praetorium of Pontius Pilate in Jerusalem on which Jesus Christ stepped on his way to trial during his Passion. The Stairs reputedly were brought to Rome by St. Helena in the fourth century. For centuries, the *Scala Sancta* has attracted Christian pilgrims who wish to honor the Passion of Jesus Christ by ascending the stairs on their knees.

Step 5: The Standard is Perfection.

day found it more uncertain, weaker, more troubled." [16]

In his classic work, *Here I Stand,* Roland Bainton wrote regarding Luther and the Confession of Sins,

> *He confessed frequently, often daily, and for as long as six hours on a single occasion. ...Luther would repeat a confession and, to be sure of including everything, would review his entire life until the confessor grew weary and exclaimed, "Man, God is not angry with you. You are angry with God. Don't you know that God commands you to hope?" In his later years, he believed he had caused permanent damage to his intestines due to his overly scrupulous monastic disciplines.* [17]

No matter what he did, he could find no peace, until one day he made an enormous discovery that fueled the Protestant Reformation and changed the world.

~~~~

---

[16] David C. Steinmetz, *Luther in Context,* (Grand Rapids: Baker, 2002), p. 2.

[17] Roland Bainton, *Here I Stand,* (Nashville: Abingdon Press, Reprint, 2013), p. 41.

Step 5: The Standard is Perfection.

Questions for Discussion:

1. In our Lutheran practice, we frown upon having eulogies at a funeral service. What is wrong with having people speak of the good life and good works done by the person who died?

2. Do you agree with the view of the popular culture that all religions should unite? Do all roads end at the same destination? Why is that not possible?

3. Should a Christian be a part of an organization, such as the Masonic Order, who teach that being a good person will merit eternal life?

Step 6:
Jesus took My Sin
and Gave me
His Righteousness!

On October 31, 1517, Martin Luther nailed his 95 Theses to the church door in Wittenberg. This date is celebrated as the beginning of the Lutheran Reformation. Yet, the content of the 95 Theses does not reflect the theology that emerged in the later confessional writings as the very impetus and heart of the Reformation. The Theses themselves were merely points of discussion and dealt primarily with the subject of the sale of indulgences and the power of the Pope to remit the penalties of those in purgatory. Luther's theology reflected in the 95 Theses is certainly not "Lutheran."

The real "shot across the bow" that fueled the Reformation and changed the face of European Christendom occurred two years later in what has been called Luther's Tower Experience. Luther makes it clear in several places that this Tower Experience, not the posting of the 95 Theses, was the pivotal event of his life.

The Tower Experience

In 1519, Luther was living in a heated room in the tower of the Black Cloister in Wittenberg, Germany, a monastery of the Augustinian hermits. Later, when all the monks had voluntarily left, it became Luther's home. It was here that he wrestled with the subject of righteousness, especially the phrase "righteousness of God" found in Romans 1:17. Paul writes in Romans 1:16-17: (KJV) "For I am not ashamed of the Gospel of Christ: for it is the power of God unto salvation to everyone that believeth; to the Jew first, and also to the Greek. For therein is the righteousness of God revealed from faith to faith: as it is written, 'The just shall live by faith.'"

Luther hated the phrase "the righteousness of God" in Romans 1:17 because he interpreted it, as did Catholic theologians, as the active righteousness of God whereby God is just in punishing sinners. He said, "I did not love, yes, I hated the righteous God who punishes sinners, and secretly, if not blasphemously, certainly murmuring greatly, I was angry with God." He meditated upon this phrase and the context day and night, and, as he put it, "Beat importunately upon Paul at that place." Finally, the light dawned, and he writes:

> *At last, by the mercy of God, meditating day and night, I gave heed to the context of the words, namely, "In it the righteousness of God is revealed, as it is written, 'He who through faith is righteous shall live.'" There I began to understand that the righteousness of God is that by which the righteous lives by a gift of God, namely by faith. And this is the meaning: the*

righteousness of God is revealed by the gospel, namely, the passive righteousness with which merciful God justifies us by faith, as it is written, "He who through faith is righteous shall live." Here I felt that I was altogether born again and had entered paradise itself through open gates. There a totally other face of the entire Scripture showed itself to me. Thereupon I ran through the Scriptures from memory. I also found in other terms an analogy, as, the work of God, that is, what God does in us, the power of God, with which he makes us strong, the wisdom of God, with which he makes us wise, the strength of God, the salvation of God, the glory of God.

And I extolled my sweetest word with a love as great as the hatred with which I had before hated the word "righteousness of God." Thus, that place in Paul was for me truly the gate to paradise. [18]

A Lesson in Grammar

The grammatical issue in Romans 1:17 is the nature of the genitive in the phrase "righteousness of God." If the phrase is translated as a *subjective genitive*, which implies possession, the righteousness of God is a quality in God. God is righteous and has

---

[18] Martin Luther, *Luther's Works*, (Philadelphia: Fortress Press, 1999), Vol. 34, pgs. 336-337.

every right to judge and punish sinners. If that is how the phrase is to be translated, it is understandable that Luther "hated the phrase 'righteousness of God.'" In Romans 1:16 the Apostle speaks of the Gospel as the "power of God for salvation." The word Gospel means "good news." How could the fact that God is righteous and has every right to punish the unrighteous sinner be good news?"

If the genitive is translated as being an *objective genitive,* it means that man becomes the object of God's righteousness or, as the *New International Version* of the Bible translates the phrase, "righteousness from God."

Consider for example the phrase "The joy of the Lord." Obviously, "joy" in that context is not subjective in the sense that God possesses joy. It is objective. The Lord gives joy to his people. In the same way, as an objective genitive, "the righteousness of God" means that God gives righteousness to his people as a gift and this is most certainly "Gospel" or good news.

This grammatical understanding of the phrase "righteousness of God" is consistent with the whole of the Apostle Paul thinking. For example, in Romans 3:21-22. he writes that now a righteousness from God, apart from law, has been made known, to which the Law and the Prophets testify. This righteousness from

Step 6: The Great Exchange

God comes through faith in Jesus Christ to all who believe. There is no difference, for all have sinned and fall short of the glory of God and are justified (made right) freely by his grace through the redemption that came by Christ Jesus.

In Philippians 3:4-9, the Apostle Paul writes:

If anyone else thinks he has reasons to put confidence in the flesh, I have more: circumcised on the eighth day, of the people of Israel, of the tribe of Benjamin, a Hebrew of Hebrews; in regard to the law, a Pharisee; as for zeal, persecuting the church; as for legalistic righteousness, faultless. But whatever was to my profit I now consider loss for the sake of Christ. What is more, I consider everything a loss compared to the surpassing greatness of knowing Christ Jesus my Lord, for whose sake I have lost all things. I consider them rubbish, that I may gain Christ and be found in him, not having a righteousness of my own that comes from the law, but that which is through faith in Christ--the righteousness that comes from God and is by faith.

The Apostle passed judgment upon everything that was a part of his former life and exchanged it for the perfect righteousness of Jesus Christ.

In 2 Corinthians 5:20 we read: "God made him who had no sin to be sin for us, so that in him we might become the righteousness of God." This verse is defined as "the great exchange." Jesus takes my sin and gives me, as a gift received by faith, His righteousness or, the righteousness of God.

In Romans 5:1: "Therefore, since we have been justified through faith, we have peace with God through our Lord Jesus Christ."

In his Tower Experience, Martin Luther uncovered the central New Testament teaching of justification by grace through faith because of Christ alone. This is the truth that changed everything and fueled the Protestant Reformation. It became and continues to be the primary controverted issue between Roman Catholics and the Lutherans.

Controversy with Rome

While Roman Catholics are Christians who focus on the Cross of Jesus Christ, they reject the clear biblical teaching concerning justification. Rome teaches the infusion of the righteousness of Christ, deposited at Baptism as an investment. Through participation in Sacraments, this righteousness is supposed to develop and grow. At death, if perfection or sainthood is not attained, the sinner is destined for purgatory where the human sinful condition is burned away and only the righteousness of

Christ remains. As one priest explained it to me, the gold is placed in the oven to be refined, and when the refiner can see his image in the gold, the individual is ready for the beatific vision or heaven and joins the communion of saints.

For Luther, the issue was not infusion but imputation. Because of the perfect righteousness of Jesus and his willingness to suffer and die on the Cross, bearing the sins of humanity, God objectively, outside of us, imputes the benefits of the righteousness of Christ to sinners who come to faith through the hearing of the Gospel.

This righteousness of Christ is not some mere abstract notion but is the actual active and passive obedience of our Lord Jesus to do the will of His Father in heaven. In his life, Jesus did everything right. When John objected to the notion of baptizing the Messiah, Jesus said it was necessary for him to fulfill all righteousness (Matthew 3:15). Jesus passively submitted to the will of His Father in heaven by being willing to go to the Cross. It is this active and passive obedience of Jesus, His fulfilling of every point of the Law, and His passive submission to death on the Cross that is imputed to the believer and received by faith.

I like to think of imputation in terms of the computer practice of blocking, copying and pasting from one source to another. God blocked and copied the record of our sins and pasted them to the account of Jesus who suffered and died on the cross, taking the punishment that we deserve; and blocked and copied the righteousness of Christ and pasted it to our account. This is Good News! In Christ Jesus, we are *perfectly righteous.*

Justification by grace through faith is the cardinal doctrine of the Christian faith. This is not the active righteousness attained by obeying the law which is something we do, but a passive righteousness, something done to us, the benefits of which are received by faith alone. This is not a "natural" righteousness, but an "alien" righteousness – the righteousness of "the Man from Heaven" - Jesus Christ.

Martin Luther writes:

> *If the doctrine of justification is lost, the whole of Christian doctrine is lost. There is no middle ground between the active righteousness of the Law and the passive righteousness of Christ. He who has strayed away from Christian righteousness will necessarily relapse into the active righteousness; that is, when he has lost Christ, he must fall into a trust in his own works.*[19]

---

[19] *Luther's Works, Lectures on Galatians,* Vol. 26, Chapters 1-4.

In Adam and in Christ

If you recall when you took the first step, we became sinners when Adam sinned, or we were born in Adam. Now we have a new designation. God included the world of sinners in Christ. We are a new creation in Christ Jesus.

The Apostle Paul writes in 1 Corinthians 1:30: "It is because of him (God) that you are in Christ Jesus, who has become for us wisdom from God--that is, our righteousness, holiness and redemption."

In 2 Corinthians 5:17: "Therefore, if anyone is in Christ, he is a new creation; the old has gone, the new has come."

In Romans 5:19: "For just as through the disobedience of the one man (Adam) the many were made sinners, so also through the obedience of the one man (Christ) the many will be made righteous."

In Adam, we are "sinners." In Christ, we are "righteous."

Now, because I am righteous in Christ, does this new life in Christ replace my old sinful nature which I received from Adam?

There are Christian groups who claim this is so. They say they don't sin anymore, but oddly, they do get older, and they do die because "the wages of sin is death."

No, you now find yourself engaged in a battle between your old life Adam and your new life in Christ.

~~~~

Questions for Discussion:

1. God, being a just God, requires payment for sin and a perfect righteousness. Only by sending Jesus, true God and true man, into the world could He accomplish that end. Can you conceive of any other way of saving the world of sinners?

2. The Apostle Paul writes in Galatians 3:23-24: "Before this faith came, we were held in custody under the Law, locked up until faith should be revealed. So, the Law became our guardian to lead us to Christ, that we might be justified by faith." What does this mean?

3. The word "forensic" is used to describe justification. What does "forensic" mean and why is it used to describe the doctrine of justification?

Step 7:
At the Same Time, I am a "Poor Miserable Sinner," I am a Redeemed, Forgiven and Righteous Saint!

On the surface, justification is not a difficult truth to grasp. It is not rocket science. Simply put, Jesus, true God and true man, took our sins upon Himself, suffered and died on the Cross, paying the just penalty so that our sins are forgiven and gave to us, as an incredible exchange, His righteousness. Jesus gets my sins, and I get His perfect righteousness. In the popular hymn we sing, "My hope is built on nothing less than Jesus' blood and righteousness." Jesus' blood and righteousness means the forgiveness of sins and justification. This is the message of the Gospel, yet it is a difficult truth to embrace. Why?

Hard to Believe

First, this Gospel is not natural truth, able to be grasped with unaided human reason. The Apostle Paul writes that man by nature is unable the grasp the things that come from the Spirit of God (1 Cor 2:14). As far as natural reason is concerned, the message of the Gospel is foolishness. 1 Corinthians 1:18 says that the message of the cross is foolishness to those who are perishing, but to us who are being saved it is the power of God. Understanding the Gospel is the result of the Holy Spirit enlightening your understanding and creating faith.

Secondly, you have the humility factor. Imagine being in a circle of friends discussing the subject of religion, and one person has the audacity to declare that he or she is perfectly righteous before God through Jesus Christ. I wonder how many "who do you think you are" looks such a person would receive?

But this is not strange. How can you say that you are perfectly righteous in Christ when you assess your life, your words, thoughts and actions? Yet, such thinking is not humility. It is rather unbelief, rejecting that which God declares to be true.

Martin Luther wrote that there is nothing laudable about that stupid, false, and harmful humility which makes you want to say that your sins prevent you from being holy.[20]

Third, it is natural to believe that being accepted by God is a reward for obeying God's Law. Children are told, "If you be a good girl or boy, you will go to heaven when you die." It fits nicely into our normal way of thinking. The preaching and teaching of the Gospel and the work of Christ runs head on into the human, natural way of thinking. It simply doesn't fit into the human mindset.

Finally, to embrace the alternative truth of justification and declare that you have the

---

[20] *Luther's Works*, Sermons on the Gospel of St. John:, 1999) John 14:27.

perfect righteousness of Jesus Christ is inconsistent with the human condition. Making such a confession to people who are familiar with your life actions, attitudes and conversation will be met with derision. How can you confess every Sunday that you are a sinner in need of forgiveness while at the same time claiming to possess the perfect righteousness of Jesus Christ?

Justification and Sanctification

Every person is born out of the root of Adam and therefore has a sinful nature. I am in Adam, and Adam is in me. I am a sinner because I was born in Adam. I daily sin much because the nature of Adam is in me.

When an unbeliever comes to faith through the hearing of the Gospel, they are joined to Jesus. They are in Christ and Christ is now in them.

There are two great truths that we cannot divide but we must distinguish. They are justification and sanctification. Justification is our position before God. It is totally the work of God. We are forgiven and righteous in Christ. This is objective truth and has nothing to do with my life or experience. So, when I declare that I am perfectly righteous in Christ, I am not talking about my life or daily experience. I am confessing what God accomplished in Christ Jesus.

Sanctification, on the other hand, defines how we live based on our position. It is a cooperative effort between you and the Holy Spirit. The Bible teaches us to live in Christ and not in Adam.

As the result of being in Adam and in Christ, while we are still upon this earth, we possess a double life. St. Paul refers to this double life as being "the old man," and "the new man," or the flesh (the sinful human nature) and the Spirit (Christ dwelling within). The life of Adam, which is our human life, will continue to adhere to us until we bury "the earthly man" in the dust from where he came. The new life of Christ which also dwells within us is an alien life. It is the life of "the heavenly man." Commenting on this double life, Martin Luther writes in his Commentary on Galatians: "There is a double life: my own which is natural or animate; and an alien life, that of Christ in me."

So, at the same time we are sinners and saints. This is expressed in the Latin phrase, *simul justus et peccator.* This does not mean that we are half sinners and half saint. In Adam, we are one hundred percent sinners, and in Christ, one hundred percent righteous.

Conflict

Because of this "double life," the normal Christian experience is conflict. One moment we may be filled with joy and peace, and at the next moment anger and frustration.

The Apostle Paul writes in Galatians 5:16: "So I say, live by the Spirit, and you will not gratify the desires of the sinful nature. For the sinful nature desires what is contrary to the Spirit, and the Spirit what is contrary to the sinful nature. They are in conflict with each other, so that you do not do what you want."

I recall an experience that took place many years ago. It had been a beautiful Sunday morning. The worship, the singing, the choir had been magnificent. I walked home from church at noon filled with joy and peace.

I greeted my wife who was busily preparing Sunday dinner.

"Wasn't that a great service?" I asked, fully expecting a confirming response.

"I didn't get anything out of it," she angrily interrupted.

"What do you mean you didn't get anything out of it? I responded incredulously. "How in the world anyone can sit in that church this morning and not get anything out of it..."

"Oh, it's easy for you," she again interrupted. "You are not stuck balancing a baby on your lap, juggling the hymnal and trying to break up the arguments between the other two. I can't understand why those kids of ours can't behave themselves in church. They are always at each other. I get so mad sometimes I could scream."

My blood began to boil. I got up from the kitchen table and marched into the living room where the Sunday papers were spread out from one end to the other. The two older kids were laid out on the floor reading the comic sections....

"What's the matter with you two?" I angrily asked. "Why can't you behave in church. You got your mother all upset."

"He keeps teasing me," my older daughter explained, pointing the finger at my oldest son who usually got the blame for most of the family squabbles, and often rightly so.

"Get out of here, both of you! I am sick and tired of looking at you! Go to your rooms!" I grabbed them both by an arm and marched them into their rooms and slammed the doors. I went back in the living room and angrily began gathering the papers together.

Amazingly, within about five minutes, my joy and peace had been replaced with anger and frustration. What a difference five minutes can make....

Normal Christian Living

This is not an abnormal situation. All Christians go through experiences of this nature. They may be joyful one moment and filled with anger and frustration the next.

Touched off by even the little negative circumstances of life, we quickly move from peace to frustration, from joy to anger, from praise and worship to arguments and personal conflicts.

Attempting to change our natural earthly life and become more loving, kind, self-controlled, patient and considerate is a hopeless task. Our human life will not cooperate with our desire for self-improvement. The Apostle Paul wrote in Romans 7:14-21.

> *We know that the law is spiritual; but I am unspiritual, sold as a slave to sin. I do not understand what I do. For what I want to do I do not do, but what I hate I do. And if I do what I do not want to do, I agree that the law is good. As it is, it is no longer I myself who do it, but it is sin living in me. I know that nothing good lives in me, that is, in my sinful nature. For I have the desire to do what is good, but I cannot carry it out. For what I do is not the good I want to do; no, the evil I do not want to do--this I keep on doing. Now if I do what I do not want to do, it is no longer I who do it, but it is sin living in me that does it.*

If a Christian does not experience conflict, it is not because he is always living according to his new life in Christ but is more likely because he simply "does what comes naturally," and lives according to the old sinful nature under the guise, "after all, I am only human." Many Christians simply give-up on themselves and say, "This is the way I am."

When we are assaulted by the temptation of the devil or when the desires of our old sinful nature fill our hearts and minds, we simply don't stand there and take it. We spring into action and confront the devil and our sinful nature with truth.

I am Baptized!

When a person is baptized as an infant or when an adult comes to faith in Jesus through the preaching of the Gospel and confirms that faith by being baptized, the statement "I am baptized" should be spoken against the temptations of the devil, the lure of the world, and the manifestation of the sinful nature. By declaring that statement, you are saying, "I am a Christian, a believer in Jesus Christ, redeemed by His precious blood and covered with his righteousness."

Tradition has it, when Martin Luther was translating the Bible into German, the language of the common man, he was assaulted by the temptations of the devil, he responded by throwing the ink bottle at the tempter and declaring, "I am baptized."

Consider these verses of Scripture:

Step 7: Saint and Sinner

The Apostle Paul writes in Romans 6:1-4: "What shall we say, then? Shall we go on sinning so that grace may increase? By no means! We died to sin; how can we live in it any longer? Or don't you know that all of us who were baptized into Christ Jesus were baptized into his death? We were therefore buried with him through baptism into death in order that, just as Christ was raised from the dead through the glory of the Father, we too may live a new life."

In Galatians 3:26, the Apostle writes: "You are all sons of God through faith in Christ Jesus, for all of you who were baptized into Christ have clothed yourselves with Christ."

Martin Luther writes, "There is a testimony in Baptism. We are baptized into Christ. His Word is present. I am baptized into Christ the Crucified."[21]

In his *Small Catechism,* Martin Luther writes concerning the significance of Baptism: "It indicates that the old Adam in us should by daily contrition and repentance be drowned and die with all sins and evil desires, and that a new man should daily emerge and arise and live before God in righteousness and purity forever."[22]

---

[21] *Luther's Works,* Lectures on 1 Timothy, 1 Timothy 2:6.
[22] *Luther's Small Catechism,* (St. Louis: Concordia Publishing House, 1986), pp. 22-23.

Some years ago, my wife and I were walking through an amusement park. I came upon the game "Whack a Mole." The player of the game is given a mallet and every time a mole pops up in one of the many holes on the board, you whack it with your mallet.

I commented, "There's Baptism."

She thought I was a little strange. But strange or not, every time the old sinful nature sticks up its ugly head, whack it with your Baptism.

Some might respond to this by saying, "Why don't you 'whack it" with the truth of the shed blood of Jesus on the Cross?"

The redemptive event of Jesus' death on the cross occurred two-thousand years ago. Jesus is no longer on the cross but is seated at the right-hand of God as King of kings and Lord of lords. So, in dealing with my sinful nature, I need to ask the question: When were the benefits of His suffering and death delivered to me? When did I confirm my faith in Jesus? When did the significance of those events enter my personal history? Some might "whack it" by naming the day they were saved, or claiming to have prayed the sinner's prayer, or invited Jesus into their hearts. I prefer to use my Baptism because I didn't do it. It was done to me.

So, whack it with your Baptism!

The Christian life is not only a defensive battle in which we are always confronting and putting down the temptations of the devil, the world and our sinful nature. We also go on the offense and seek to live and walk in Christ Jesus.

But before we do that, we need to understand what God has given to us in the person of Christ Jesus. Because I am unable by my own effort to be a more loving, forgiving, patient or joyful person does not mean that those attributes are unavailable. I just need to know where to find them so that they may be a part of my life and experience.

~~~~

Questions for Discussion:

1. Everyone by nature has mood swings: happy one day, miserable the next. How is the designation "at the same time I am a sinner and righteous" different?

2. Everything God has accomplished for us is *extra nos,* meaning "outside of us." *Mysticism* is the practice of "looking inward" to find spiritual reality. If we choose to look inward, what must we always discover?

3. Contrary to the Roman Catholic definition of a saint, Martin Luther said that every Christian is a saint. Why is that true?

Step 8:
Our Lord Jesus Christ
is the Singular Solution
to the Human Dilemma!

It wasn't too many years ago when we needed a bunch of electronic equipment to do the things we wanted to do. We needed a telephone to communicate. We needed a camera to take pictures, and a video camera to take movies. We needed a computer to get on the Internet and send e-mail. We needed a game player to play games. Now we have smartphones, and all the other "stuff" has become obsolete. A smartphone loaded with "apps" provides everything we need. For this reason, we guard our smartphones. Think of everything you lose, if you lose your smartphone.

In the same way, God does not grant to us a host of different spiritual benefits. God does not offer to us forgiveness, righteousness, love, peace, and joy as separate entities. God has only given to us one thing: His Son Jesus Christ. Like a smartphone, in Christ are all the spiritual blessings and benefits of life and salvation. Everything we need is in Christ. If we lose Christ, we lose everything.

Everything in Christ

The Bible says: "Praise be to the God and Father of our Lord Jesus Christ, who has blessed us in the heavenly realms, with every spiritual blessing in Christ." (Ephesians 1:3)

"It is because of Him that you are in Christ Jesus, who has become for us wisdom from God, that is, our righteousness, holiness and redemption. (1 Corinthians 1:30)

"That they may know the mystery of God, namely Christ, in whom are hidden all the treasures of wisdom and knowledge.... So then, just as you received Christ Jesus as Lord, continue to live in him, rooted and built up in him...and you have been given fullness in Christ." (Colossians 2:2,3,6,7,10)

"His divine power has given us everything we need for life and godliness through our knowledge of him who has called us by his own glory and goodness. (2 Peter 1:3)

In his classic book *The Normal Christian Life,* Chinese pastor and evangelist Watchman Nee writes:

> *God will not give me humility or patience or holiness or love as separate gifts of his grace. He is not a retailer dispensing grace to us in packets, measuring out some patience to the impatient, some love to the unloving, some meekness to the proud, in quantities that we take and work on as a kind of capital. He has given only one gift to meet our need: His Son Christ Jesus. As I look to Him to live out His life in me, He will be humble and patient and loving and everything else I need in my stead.... It does not matter what your personal deficiency, or*

106

whether it be a hundred and one different things, God has always one sufficient answer, His Son Jesus Christ, and He is the answer to every human need.[23]

In describing the sufficiency of the person of Jesus Christ, Martin Luther wrote: "For in the person of Christ, there is everything, and without the Son, everything is lost. Therefore, it is no small matter that without the Son, we should seek nothing and will find nothing in heaven nor on earth, for then all is lost."[24]

It is very important for our understanding and experience of the Christian life that we recognize that all Christian benefits, gifts, and fruit are found in the person of Christ Jesus. If we desire the forgiveness of sins and a righteousness that is acceptable to God, God gives us Jesus. If we seek peace, joy, and love God gives us Jesus. If we desire comfort in the midst of sorrow, hope when things look hopeless, assurance when plagued by doubt, and contentment through the changing scenes of life, God gives us Jesus.

In Galatians 3:27, Paul writes: "All of you who were baptized have clothed yourself with Christ." When we came to faith in the Lord

---

[23] Watchman Nee, *The Normal Christian* Life, (Fort Washington: Christian Literature Crusade, 1961), pg. 127.

[24] Werner Elert, *The Structure of Lutheranism,* (St. Louis: Concordia Publishing House, 1962), pg. 67

Jesus, and were baptized, all the benefits found in Christ Jesus became our possession. We have His peace and joy, His righteousness and holiness. His love is shed abroad in our hearts through the Holy Spirit. In fact, the Bible tells us that in Christ we are complete and fulfilled. The Gospel of Jesus Christ is truly a message of Good News. We discover everything "in Christ," and will find nothing "outside of Christ."

"Christ is all and in all!"

In the Gospel of John, our Lord Jesus speaks of himself as being the very essence of all the blessings and promises of God. "He is the Way, the Truth, and the Life." At Lazarus' tomb, Jesus did not speak of resurrection as being a reward for a life well-lived. He said, "I am the Resurrection." After feeding the 5000, he offered himself as being the very bread that came down from heaven. He is the light of the World. He is the water of Life. He is the Good Shepherd. In Him was Life and the Life was the Light of men."

Martin Luther described this reality in his 1535 commentary on Galatians: "Because He lives in me, whatever grace, righteousness, life, peace and salvation there is in me all Christ's; nevertheless, it is mine as well by the cementing and attachment that are through faith, by which we become as one body in the Spirit."[25]

Because every Christian has Christ dwelling within through faith, it must therefore follow that every Christian possesses God's everything. While it is true that some Christians, because of personal deficiency and need, have seemingly appropriated more of the blessings that have been provided in Christ than have other Christians, but they dare not declare or even remotely suggest, "I have something you don't have."

For example, a person who has passed through times of grief and turned in faith to Jesus, discovered in Him the source of deep, abiding comfort. He is thereby enabled to declare, "Christ is my comfort!" One who possibly has not shared the same need might not have discovered the same provision in Christ. This does not mean that such provision is not already his possession, ready to be grasped by faith. For if we have Christ and have put on Christ, we have God's everything.

On Account of Christ

The Latin phrase *propter Christum* means "on account of Christ." We can add that phrase after every Christian issue. Do I have

---

[25] Martin Luther, 1535 *Commentary on Galatians,* p. 170.

forgiveness, righteousness, eternal life in heaven, peace, joy, love and hope? Yes, *propter Christum*, on account of Christ.

I have taught people to answer the following questions in this simple manner, "Are your sins forgiven and do you have eternal life?" YES, because I have Christ! "Are you perfectly righteous before God and can stand confidently before Him?" YES, because I have Christ. "Do you have love, peace, and joy in this world?" YES, because I have Christ. "Do you have eternal life in heaven" YES, because I have Christ.

What a simple yet profound confession, "I have Christ!"

The Apostle Paul writes in Colossians 2:6: "So then, just as you received Christ Jesus as Lord, continue to live in him, rooted and built up in him, strengthened in the faith as you were taught, and overflowing with thankfulness."

Yes, I have Christ, so how do I live in him?

~~~~

Questions for Discussion:

1. There are all kinds of human emotional issues. What are some of the solutions offered by the world?

2. Some Christian psychologists have said that the Bible does not deal with all human issues and must be supplemented with the findings of psychology. Is it one thing to say that the Bible is an insufficient solution and another thing to say that Jesus is an insufficient solution?

3. Claiming that Jesus is the singular solution does not rule out legitimate human emotional issues that require the findings of psychology or prescribing medication. How might we discern whether a person's lack of peace, joy and hope requires Valium rather than Jesus?

Step 9:
Living and Walking
In Christ Jesus

The Bible says in 1 John 1:8-10: "If we claim to be without sin, we deceive ourselves and the truth is not in us. If we confess our sins, he is faithful and just and will forgive us our sins and purify us from all unrighteousness. If we claim we have not sinned, we make him out to be a liar and his word has no place in our lives.

An important part of living the Christian life is to examine ourselves and confess our sins to God, to repent and receive his forgiveness. In his *Significance of Baptism,* Martin Luther spoke of daily contrition and repentance. But before I can do that, I need to identify my sins.

For many Christians, a sin is breaking one of the Ten Commandments. If they examine themselves and conclude that they have externally obeyed the Ten Commandment, they think of themselves as being without sin. They have nothing to confess.

In His *Sermon on the Mount,* Jesus expanded the Ten Commandments to include, not merely the external acts, but the attitudes of the heart. Jesus said, "You have heard that it was said to the people long ago, `Do not murder, and anyone who murders will be subject to judgment.' But I tell you that anyone who is angry with his brother will be subject to judgment." "You have heard that it was said, `Do not commit adultery.' But I tell you that anyone who looks at a woman lustfully has already committed adultery with her in his heart: (Matthew 5:21-22,27-28)'"

In Matthew 15:19, Jesus said, "For out of the heart come evil thoughts, murder, adultery, sexual immorality, theft, false testimony, slander."

A sin against God is not merely defined by externally disobeying one of the Ten Commandment but includes all the thoughts, attitudes and actions that proceed from our sinful nature.

Works and Fruit

As I have said before, we have two sources of life identified as Adam and Christ, the "old man" and the "new man," or the "flesh" and the "Spirit." The one produces various works while the other produces various fruit. It is not difficult to determine the source of your thoughts, words or actions. The Apostle Paul writes in Galatians 5:19-22:

The acts of the sinful nature are obvious: sexual immorality, impurity and debauchery; idolatry and witchcraft; hatred, discord, jealousy, fits of rage, selfish ambition, dissensions, factions and envy; drunkenness, orgies, and the like. I warn you, as I did before, that those who live like this will not inherit the kingdom of

God. But the fruit of the Spirit is love, joy, peace, patience, kindness, goodness, faithfulness, gentleness and self-control.

If you examine your life and discover envy, selfish ambition and jealousy, even though these attitudes are not forbidden in the Ten Commandments, they proceed from the sinful nature and are sins. If you are involved in a group where there is discord, factions, and dissension, it is not difficult to arrive at the conclusion that the group is motivated by the old sinful nature.

There is one statement in that section from Galatians that needs to be clarified. The Apostle wrote: "Those who live like this will not inherit the kingdom of God."

If the Apostle is directing this statement at unbelievers and false Christians, it is, as Martin Luther points out, intended to "frighten some of them thoroughly, so that they would begin to battle against the works of the flesh by the Spirit and stop performing them."[26] Luther is identifying the Kingdom of God as heaven.

But if the Apostle is writing this statement to Christians, this cannot mean that when your actions are motivated by the old sinful nature you will not go to heaven. If that were the case, no one would make it because we all, from time

---

[26] Martin Luther, *1535 Commentary on Galatians,* pg. 92.

to time, manifest the works of the sinful nature, especially since the Apostle added the phrase "and the like." The list is endless. For example, for a long time I lived immersed in self-pity. That is obviously a work of the sinful nature, but at the time, I did not identify it as a sin. Does that mean that I would not go to heaven because I felt sorry for myself? Jesus died on the cross so that the sins that emerge from our sinful nature would be forgiven.

In Romans 14:17, Paul identifies the Kingdom of God as "righteousness, peace, and joy in the Holy Spirit." I believe that Paul is saying that if we live according to the old sinful nature we will miss out on our inheritance in the Kingdom of God. In other words, we will be miserable and have no joy or peace.

The Fruit of the Spirit

Alternatively, if we live and walk in Christ Jesus, according to the "Spirit" and not the flesh or sinful nature, we will produce the fruit of the Spirit. Love, joy, peace, patience will be a part of our life and experience.

Our Lord Jesus said in John 15, "I am the vine; you are the branches. If a man remains in me and I in him, he will bear much fruit; apart from me you can do nothing."

For a long time, I struggled with the issue of the Christian life. The issue was not the external breaking of the Ten Commandments, but the thoughts, words and attitudes that emerged from my sinful nature: selfish ambition, worry, self-pity, anger, bitterness, frustration and the like. I knew, after studying Romans and Galatians, these attitudes were sins, they were a part of my sinful nature. I knew how God wanted me to live and act, but I could not do it. Even though I knew the law, what is right and wrong, good and bad, I did not have the power to do it. The law is powerless to change my sinful nature.

One afternoon I was standing at my patio door looking at the trees in my backyard as I meditated upon the vine/branch teaching of Jesus from John 15. It was wintertime. The variety of oak trees in my yard did not lose their leaves. Instead, their leaves simply turned brown. For all practical purposes, the trees were dead. The thought struck me, "How do those trees get rid of their brown leaves and get new ones?"

I answered my own question by thinking, "They wait until springtime. When the sap comes up out of the roots, it flows into the branches. The old leaves fall off and the new buds appear.'

I came to see that the Christian life was not "my life," but was the life of Christ Jesus dwelling in me. In the same way that the life of the tree is found in the sap which flows into its branches, so the life of the Christian is found in Christ Jesus who dwells within.

I realized that God had not given me a whole list of things to do and not to do. While the Bible certainly gives many such instructions, God never intended for me to fulfill them by way of willpower and resolutions. God gave me one task: *to abide in Christ Jesus*! I had been concerned with getting rid of the old leaves in my life, and I wanted to bear fruit, but I didn't know how to do it. I was trying to shake off the leaves using my own willpower but without success. This produced great frustration. My eyes were opened to the truth that I had to stay close to Jesus, and His life in me would do the rest.

The Apostle Paul writes in Colossians 2:6-7: "So then, just as you received Christ Jesus as Lord, continue to live in him, rooted and built up in him."

How to Abide in Christ

The "how to" instructions for abiding in Christ or living according to the Spirit and not according to the sinful nature are things we are able to do. They are instructions or principles pertaining to life. For example, how do you deal with hunger? Eat! How to you deal with thirst? Drink some water! How do you overcome fatigue? Take a nap or get a good night's sleep! These are things we obviously can do.

In the same manner, the instructions in the New Testament for abiding in Christ, or how the Apostle defines it as "living in the Spirit," are things we can do. They are also instructions or principles pertaining to life, our life in Christ. We read in Romans 8:1-2: "Therefore, there is now no condemnation for those who are in Christ Jesus, because through Christ Jesus the law of the Spirit of life set me free from the law of sin and death." The word "law" in these verses means "principle," similar to speaking of the "law of gravity." Instructions for living in Christ are "principles" pertaining to life.

For example, consider the law of gravity. There is also a law of physics or a principle defining the function of a parachute. So, if I jump out of an airplane, the principle of a parachute will set me free from the full effect of the law of gravity.

In the same, abiding in Christ sets us free from the works of the sinful nature.

So, how do we abide in Christ or live and walk in the Spirit?

Confess the Truth: Many within the church today only confess half-truths. Many of us Lutherans, for example, in our weekly confession, are very willing to confess and acknowledge our sin and failure, but often neglect to confess the righteousness God has

119

granted to us in Christ Jesus. Others, freely confess who they are in Christ, but fail to recognize that they are still dragging old Adam around with them. A true Christian confession is not one or the other, but "both and."

The Bible says that we have a double life. On the one hand, God says in His Word, "Because you are born in Adam, you are a sinner. Your human nature has been corrupted and perverted by sin. You are going to die." As we examine our own hearts, we confess, "I agree. I am a poor, miserable, wretched sinner!" But this is not the extent of our confession. God also affirms in the Gospel: "Because I have included you in my Son Jesus Christ, you are a forgiven, redeemed, righteous, saint!" Standing firmly and confidently upon the truth of God's Word, we also confess, "I agree. I am forgiven and righteous in Christ. I believe your Word and promise."

Our confession is determined by where we choose to look. This is a very important truth. If we look at ourselves, we see our sin. If we look at Jesus, we see our righteousness. It all depends on our focus.

The Word of God: Confessing and declaring the truth of God's Word is a vital ingredient in living the Christian life and learning to live in the Spirit. The Word of God is the means for the working of the Holy Spirit in our hearts. By speaking to ourselves the message of God's grace, love and forgiveness in Christ the very presence of the Holy Spirit is stirred within us.

Martin Luther writes: "I still constantly find that when I am without the Word, Christ is gone, yes, and so are joy and the Spirit. But as soon as I look at a psalm or a passage of Scripture, it so shines and burns into my heart that I gain a different spirit and mind. Moreover, I know that everybody may daily experience this in his own life."

The confessing of key Bible passages which declare the results of what God has accomplished in Christ is vitally important to our living and walking in the Spirit. Much of what we have discussed can be found in the first eight chapters of Book of Romans. Here are some key verses from Romans that I have found very useful:

1:16-17: "I am not ashamed of the gospel, because it is the power of God for the salvation of everyone who believes: first for the Jew, then for the Gentile. For in the gospel a righteousness from God is revealed, a righteousness that is by faith from first to last, just as it is written: 'The righteous will live by faith.'"

3:21-24: "But now a righteousness from God, apart from law, has been made known, to which the Law and the Prophets testify. This righteousness from God comes through faith in

Jesus Christ to all who believe. There is no difference, for all have sinned and fall short of the glory of God and are justified freely by his grace through the redemption that came by Christ Jesus."

5:1: "Therefore, since we have been justified through faith, we have peace with God through our Lord Jesus Christ."

5:12: "Therefore, just as sin entered the world through one man, and death through sin, and in this way, death came to all men, because all sinned."

5:19: "For just as through the disobedience of the one man the many were made sinners, so also through the obedience of the one man the many will be made righteous."

6:1-4: "What shall we say, then? Shall we go on sinning so that grace may increase? By no means! We died to sin; how can we live in it any longer? Or don't you know that all of us who were baptized into Christ Jesus were baptized into his death? We were therefore buried with him through baptism into death in order that, just as Christ was raised from the dead through the glory of the Father, we too may live a new life."

6:23: "For the wages of sin is death, but the gift of God is eternal life in Christ Jesus our Lord."

7:14-20: "For what I do is not the good I want to do; no, the evil I do not want to do--this

I keep on doing. Now if I do what I do not want to do, it is no longer I who do it, but it is sin living in me that does it."

8:1-4: "Therefore, there is now no condemnation for those who are in Christ Jesus, because through Christ Jesus the law of the Spirit of life set me free from the law of sin and death. For what the law was powerless to do in that it was weakened by the sinful nature, God did by sending his own Son in the likeness of sinful man to be a sin offering. And so he condemned sin in sinful man, in order that the righteous requirements of the law might be fully met in us, who do not live according to the sinful nature but according to the Spirit."

8:28: "And we know that in all things God works for the good of those who love him, who have been called according to his purpose."

8:31-39: (These are power packed verses.) What, then, shall we say in response to this? If God is for us, who can be against us? He who did not spare his own Son, but gave him up for us all--how will he not also, along with him, graciously give us all things? Who will bring any charge against those whom God has chosen? It is God who justifies. Who is he that condemns? Christ Jesus, who died--more than that, who was raised to life--is at the right hand of God and is also interceding for us. Who shall separate us from the love of Christ? Shall trouble or hardship or persecution or famine or nakedness or danger or sword....No, in all these things we are more than conquerors through him who loved us. For I am convinced that neither death nor life, neither angels nor demons, neither the present nor the future, nor any powers, neither height nor depth, nor anything else in all creation, will be able to separate us from the love of God that is in Christ Jesus our Lord."

Use these verses. Make a list of them. Speak them to yourself. If possible, memorize them or portions of them. They are powerful means for living and walking in Christ Jesus.

The Lord's Supper: The Gospels of Matthew, Mark and Luke and 1 Corinthians state that our Lord Jesus Christ, the same night in which He was betrayed, took bread and when He had given thanks, He broke it and gave it to His disciples saying: 'Take, eat; this is My body, which is given for you. This do in remembrance of Me." In the same way also, He took the cup after supper, gave thanks, and gave it to them saying: "Drink of it all of you; this cup is the New Testament in My blood, which is shed for you and for many, for the remission of sins. This do as often as you drink it, in remembrance of Me."

Ever since Jesus spoke those words and instituted the Lord's Supper, Christians, in their Sunday morning worship gatherings, have followed the words of Jesus and did what He instructed them to do.

The Lord's Supper also goes by the name of Holy Communion, the Sacrament of the Altar and the Eucharist, a word derived from the Greek for "giving thanks."

Among Christians, there are different interpretations of what Jesus meant when he said, "This is my body," and "This is my blood." Roman Catholics teach a view called "transubstantiation," meaning that when Jesus' Words of Institution are spoken over the bread and wine, the bread actually, in substances, changes into the body of Christ and the wine, in substance, changes into the blood of Christ. Reformed Churches, or those who follow the teachings of John Calvin, teach that Jesus is spiritually present in the Lord's Supper. Many other Protestant churches believe that the bread and grape juice, rather than wine, merely represents the body and blood of Jesus.

It is interesting to note that Welch's grape juice was originally manufactured to be used as a substitute for wine in the Lord's Supper, even though the Bible clearly states that Jesus used wine.

Martin Luther, in his *Small Catechism,* defined the Lord's Supper or the Sacrament of the Altar as the true body and blood of our Lord Jesus Christ under the bread and wine, instituted by Christ Himself for us Christians to eat and drink."[27]

The correct biblical understanding is that the body and blood of Christ is joined to the bread and the wine. The Apostle Paul wrote in 1 Corinthians 10:16: "Is not the cup of thanksgiving for which we give thanks a participation in the blood of Christ? And is not the bread that we break a participation in the body of Christ?"

The word translated "participation" in the *New International Version* of the Bible means "communion" or "fellowship." The Body of Christ is "in communion" with the bread and the Blood of Christ with the cup.

The Apostle writes 1 Corinthians 11:27, "Therefore whoever eats this bread or drinks this cup of the Lord in an unworthy manner will be guilty of the body and blood of the Lord." Notice he is not guilty of the bread or wine, but "the body and blood of the Lord."

The Lord's Supper is for Christians only. I am not a Christian because I receive the Lord's Supper. I receive the Lord's Supper because I am a Christian. In that Supper of the Lord we again receive the forgiveness of our sins and are strengthened in our faith. We can go out into the world assured that we are a part of

---

[27] *Luther's Small Catechism*, p. 28

God's people and that Jesus gave His life for us.

Since participating in the Lord's Supper is am expression of unity, we "commune" with those with whom we are in agreement.

Being a part of a Christian Church where the Word of God is properly taught and where Baptism and the Lord's Supper are administered according to the command of Jesus is vital for our daily walk with the Lord.

Beginning with the Mind: Every work of the flesh or the sinful nature begins between he ears. This is probably the most important truth I have learned concerning living the Christian life. Consider these verses:

Romans 8:5-8: "Those who live according to the sinful nature have their minds set on what that nature desires; but those who live in accordance with the Spirit have their minds set on what the Spirit desires. The mind of sinful man is death, but the mind controlled by the Spirit is life and peace; the sinful mind is hostile to God. It does not submit to God's law, nor can it do so. Those controlled by the sinful nature cannot please God."

Romans 12:1-2: "Therefore, I urge you, brothers, in view of God's mercy, to offer your bodies as living sacrifices, holy and pleasing to God--this is your spiritual act of worship. Do not conform any longer to the pattern of this world but be transformed by the renewing of your mind."

Ephesians 4:22-24: You were taught, with regard to your former way of life, to put off the old man, which is being corrupted by its deceitful desires; to be made new in the attitude of your minds; and to put on the new man, created to be like God in true righteousness and holiness."

Colossians 3:1-2: "Since, then, you have been raised with Christ, set your hearts on things above, where Christ is seated at the right hand of God. Set your minds on things above, not on earthly things."

Philippians 4:8: "Finally, brothers, whatever is true, whatever is noble, whatever is right, whatever is pure, whatever is lovely, whatever is admirable--if anything is excellent or praiseworthy--think about such things."

Every sin, every temptation, every work of the sinful nature begins with a thought.

Many years ago, a ten-year-old girl, living in our immediate neighborhood, was kidnapped while walking home from school. Thus, the children in the local schools were instructed to be careful walking home, and to avoid contact with strangers. My youngest son Danny, who was also ten years old at the time, became gripped and immobilized by fear. He could not sleep nights. He couldn't eat. He refused to go outside and play. Even though his school was only two blocks from home, we had to drive him to school every morning and pick him up immediately in front of the school door in the afternoon.

This went on for several days. No matter how much we tried to convince him that, while he should be cautious and that his fear was proper in the light of the circumstances, it was magnified beyond a normal response, nothing worked. We used the other children in his class as examples of being cautious without being gripped with fear, but it made no difference. Finally, one evening, before he went to sleep, I taught him the principle of Romans 8:5-6. I instructed him to "kick-out of his mind" any thoughts of fear that sought entrance and to redirect his thoughts and begin singing "Jesus loves me this I know." We prayed that Jesus would fill his mind with good things.

The next morning, he came downstairs, ready to go to school, and announced in his usual happy-go-lucky fashion, "You don't have to drive me this morning. Fear tried to get in, but I kicked it out and sang `Jesus Loves Me.' It hasn't come back!"

One day I had lunch with a good friend of mine at the Holiday Inn in Grand Rapids. I enjoyed this man's company because we were both seeking to grow in our relationship with the Lord Jesus. So, we had much to talk about and would meet for lunch quite often.

While we were eating, we noticed that there was much activity taking place around the indoor pool which was adjacent to the restaurant, but we did not pay it much attention.

As we left the restaurant, we decided to walk down one of the long motel corridors to the back-parking lot where we had left our cars. There was much commotion in the narrow hallway, especially at the entrance to the swimming pool. Drawing closer, we found ourselves passing between two lines of beautiful, bikini-clad models. The commotion at the pool had been a fashion show. As we gingerly "walked the line" between the two rows of exposed flesh, I heard my friend mumbling under his breath:

"Thank you, Lord Jesus. You certainly are a wonderful creator. You do all things well...." I couldn't help but laugh.

As we got out to the parking lot, I questioned him, "We're walking between all these beautiful models and you're declaring the goodness of God?"

With a big grin, he replied, "It sure beats lust!!"

Worry, anxiety, fear, lust, self-pity are mental attitudes. They seek to gain the control of our minds. In so doing, they pollute and defile us. My son Danny was gripped by an unnatural fear. My friend and I could have easily fallen prey to lust and sexual desire. As the result of re-directing the mind to Jesus, we are enabled to be set free from the thoughts that emerge from the sinful nature.

In quoting a work by St. Jerome, Martin Luther wrote, "You cannot prevent the birds from flying over your head, but you can certainly keep them from building a nest in your hair."[28]

Luther further wrote, "Thinking must be turned in another direction and Christ must be thought of so that you may say, Christ lives!"[29]

Some years ago, I led a three-night seminar in Toledo, Ohio. I was met at the airport by a middle-aged couple. As we drove away from the airport, their first words related the story of the tragic death of their only daughter in an automobile accident two years before. They confessed, "We have never gotten over it."

The second evening of the seminar, I spoke about responding to worry, fear and sadness by setting our minds upon the promises of God and abiding in Christ.

The next evening on the way back to the airport, they said, "By putting into practice what you taught, last night was the first good night's sleep we have had in two years."

---

[28] Martin Luther, *Luther's Works,* Vol. 42, p.73
[29] Plass, 1345

Rejoice in the Lord! The Bible tells us in Philippians 4:4: to rejoice in the Lord always. Our joy in all situations of life is directly in proportion to our faith in the Word and promise of God. Martin Luther said, "You have as much laughter as you have faith." And again, "We can mark our lack of faith by our joy; for our joy must necessarily be as great as our faith."[30]

In Ephesians, the Apostle Paul clearly defines the joyful stance of the Christian. He writes: "Do not get drunk on wine, which leads to debauchery. Instead be filled with the Spirit. Speak to one another with psalms, hymns, and spiritual songs. Sing and make music in your heart to the Lord, always giving thanks to God the Father for everything in the name of our Lord Jesus Christ." (5:18-19)

From the Word of God, it is very clear that singing songs of praise and worship is a vital ingredient in living in the Spirit and abiding in Christ. Martin Luther thought very highly of music and singing in the life of the Christian and placed it right behind theology in importance. He said, "I place music next to theology and give it the highest praise." He wrote a great deal about the positive results of singing songs of praise and worship. In a letter

---

[30] Plass, *What Luther Says,* p. 69.

to a Matthias Weller, a man known for brooding, Luther wrote:

> *When sadness comes to you and threatens to gain the upper hand, then say: Come, I must play our Lord Christ a song on the organ for Scripture teaches me that he loves to hear joyful song and stringed instruments. And strike the keys with a will and sing out until the thoughts disappear....If the devil returns and suggests cares or sad thoughts, then defend yourselves with a will and say: Get out, devil, I must now sing and play to my Lord Christ.*[31]

When the desires of our sinful human nature cry out for our attention and when the devil stands ready to bring us into worry, fear, depression, self-pity and the like, there is no better means for us to abide in Christ than to confess the truth of the promises of God and sing a song of praise and worship to Jesus. Anger, fear, bitterness, lust and envy must give way to the joyful sounds of praise and worship. You may not be familiar with a host of traditional hymns or contemporary worship music. For my son Dan, the simple words of "Jesus loves me this I know, for the Bible tells me so" worked, and it will work for you too.

---

[31] Plass, pg. 983.

If it wasn't for the adverse situations of life, the attitudes of other people, the plans that go awry, the circumstances which are beyond our control, living and walking in Christ Jesus would not be very difficult. Anyone can rejoice in a joyful situation. Anyone can be happy when everything is going according to our plans and purposes. Anyone can love lovable people. Anyone can be at peace amid serenity.

But, living and walking in the Spirit and abiding in Christ Jesus is the most productive of good fruit in the midst of adversity. The fruit of the Spirit is not a gift. It is worked in us as we abide in Christ when everything is seemingly going wrong.

I heard of a man who prayed for more patience. A few days later, his secretary quit, and he was "blessed" with a totally inept temp. God had answered his prayer. He would either get the fruit of patience or live in frustration.

In Philippians 4:11-13, the Apostle Paul writes: "I have learned to be content whatever the circumstances. I know what it is to be in need, and I know what it is to have plenty. I have learned the secret of being content in any and every situation, whether well fed or hungry, whether living in plenty or in want. I can do everything through him who gives me strength."

In Acts 16 we read the story of Paul and Silas who had been beaten and thrown into jail at Philippi, even though they had done nothing wrong. In fact, Paul was a Roman citizen who was not given a fair hearing. They were being punished because they delivered a girl from demonic bondage. They had every reason to complain and gripe about their situation and feel sorry for themselves. God had seemingly let them down.

Instead, the Bible tells us that they were singing hymns and psalms of praise. They knew the Word and promises of God. They were being led by the Holy Spirit and God would work everything out according to his will and purpose. By singing hymns of praise, they retained their peace of mind, their joy, and emotional stability amid a negative situation. As a bonus, God opened the prison doors.

There is a warped sense of enjoyment associated with being miserable and having other people know that you are miserable. "Ol' Adam" can become a very good and comfortable friend. I used to be a part of a clergy "support group" which I later identified as the 4P Club: the poor pastor's pity party. We would get together every few weeks and rehearse our personal travail, ego afflictions and insecurities associated with the task of "suffering through the heat of the day" in graciously serving the Lord. The last thing we wanted to hear was somebody instructing us to get our minds off ourselves, claim the promises of God and rejoice in the Lord. Yet, that was the very thing we needed to hear.

In teaching these truths for the past forty years, I have encountered numerous people who refused to embrace them because, for some reason, they enjoyed being miserable.

Every night, before I go to sleep, I instruct Alexa, the woman somehow contained within my *Echo Dot,* to play "relaxing piano music, greatest hymns," and I go to sleep in peace. Try it. You'll like it.

The Apostle Paul summarizes the Christian life in Colossians 3:16-17: "Let the word of Christ dwell in you richly as you teach and admonish one another with all wisdom, and as you sing psalms, hymns and spiritual songs with gratitude in your hearts to God. And whatever you do, whether in word or deed, do it all in the name of the Lord Jesus, giving thanks to God the Father through him."

~~~~

Questions for Discussion:

1. Why is it easier to confess, "I am a sinner," rather than to say, "I am righteous in Christ?" Confession means "to speak with." We "speak with" and agree with what God says. What does God say about our condition?

2. Over the next couple days, discern how much of your emotional life or the attitudes of your heart are determined by what is going on between your ears. Are you allowing the "birds that fly over your head to make a nest in your hair?"

3. The Apostle Paul writes in Philippians 4:4: "Rejoice in the Lord always. I will say it again: Rejoice!" Paul does not say, "Rejoice in the Lord when everything is going well, and you have reason to rejoice." Why can a Christian rejoice in the Lord always?

Step 10:
Heaven is not my GOAL!
It is my DESTINATION!
I know the WAY!

I was invited to fill in for a pastor who was on vacation and conduct his two Sunday morning services and do the Bible Class. I decided to teach in Bible class some of the biblical principles for abiding in Christ.

After I finished teaching, I asked, "Are there any questions?"

One man raised his hand and asked,

"Do I have to abide in Christ to get to heaven?"

"No," I replied. "Heaven is a gift based on what Jesus did for you by suffering and dying on the cross."

"Good," he replied, somewhat relieved. "All I want to do is go to heaven."

I was tempted to respond by saying, "If all you want to do is go to heaven, why don't you die and get it over with?" but I figured that would merely be a manifestation of my reactionary sinful nature.

I did inform that him that "abiding in Christ" was not my idea but the directive of Jesus.

Heaven is not a Goal

It is understandable that for many Christians going to heaven is their singular desire. Death is the ultimate concern. We read in Hebrews 9:27: "Just as people are destined to die once, and after that to face judgment." It is perhaps the only question that remains unanswered.

Everyone wants to secure their future. While younger folks seek job security, the older generation is continually bombarded with television commercials asking the question of whether you have sufficient resources for your retirement.

So, people make plans and set goals for their lives. They go to college and get a degree with the hope of landing a job that will provide financial security. A portion of their income is set aside for social security and retirement programs. The goal is security. But through it all, there remains the burning issue of death, and built into the human psych is the hope of life after death. If there is no life after death, life itself becomes meaningless, or as Shakespeare put it in *Macbeth:*

> *Tomorrow, and tomorrow, and tomorrow, creeps in this petty pace from day to day to the last syllable of recorded time, and all our yesterdays have lighted fools the way to dusty death. Out, out, brief candle! Life's but a walking shadow, a poor player that struts and frets his hour upon the stage and then is heard no more. It is a tale told by an idiot, full of sound and fury, signifying nothing.*

Religion answers the ultimate question of what is going to happen after death. Those concerned about their eternal future become religious. Every world religion has an answer for the ultimate question, and in all cases, except for Christianity, attaining the goal of heaven, nirvana, or paradise involves something you have to do.

If someone says, "All I want to do is go to heaven," it is obvious that the issue remains unsettled. They are uncertain whether they will attain the goal of going to heaven. If you ask them whether they are going to heaven after they die, they will usually respond, "I sure hope so."

For a Christian, heaven is not a goal but a destination. Consider the difference.

If you go out to the airport and board a flight for New York, and when you reach thirty-thousand feet, the pilot comes on the speaker and says, "Our goal this afternoon is to get you to New York."

Would you want to have him as a pilot? For all you know, you may land and be in Cuba. New York is not the goal. It is the destination, because the pilot knows the way.

In the upper room on the night before he went to the cross, Jesus told his disciples that He was going away. He said, "In my Father's house are many rooms; if it were not so, I would have told you. I am going there to prepare a place for you. And if I go and prepare a place for you, I will come back and take you to be with me that you also may be where I am. You know the way to the place where I am going." But Thomas said to him, 'Lord, we don't know where you are going, so how can we know the way?' Jesus answered, 'I am the way and the truth and the life. No one comes to the Father except through me." (John 14:1-6)

Jesus is the Way! If the Holy Spirit has brought you to faith through the hearing of the Gospel, you have Christ, and if you have Christ, you have eternal life in heaven, because Jesus is the Way. Heaven is not your goal. It is your destination.

Martin Luther wrote:

> *If we want to feel assured of reaching heaven, we must have a sure way and road to travel; for there can be no more than one right way and road. And such a way is indicated only in God's Word. Christ the Lord Himself is the only Way and the right Road on which our heart can and must rely and depend. Therefore, Christ concludes: "He who would be safe and not meet eternal loss and ruin, let him give ear to Me*

alone; and let Me impress these words deeply: 'I am the Way.'[32]

Because God has granted to us the benefits of the work of Christ, his shed blood and perfect righteousness, heaven is not our goal. Rather, it is our destination, a gift from God. Our goal is to live each day in relationship with our Lord Jesus Christ.

Eternal Security?

The Roman Catholic Church teaches that a person cannot be certain of their eternal life in heaven. If a person commits or is living in some mortal sin[33] and dies before having the opportunity to repent, confess that sin and receive the Sacrament of Penance, they will go to hell. They accused Luther and the Reformers of teaching an "easy believeism:" regardless of what you do, faith saves you.

In response to this, Philip Melanchthon wrote in the *Apology to the Augsburg Confession,*

---

[32] Martin Luther, *Luther's Works: Sermons on the Gospel of St. John,* Vol. 24, John 14:7

[33] A mortal sin in Catholic theology is a wrongful act that condemn a person to Hell after death if unforgiven. These sins are considered "mortal" because they constitute a rupture in a person's link to God's saving grace. A "venial" sin is a lesser sin because it does not cause a person to separate from God.

Step 10: I Know the Way!

But we are talking about a faith that is not an idle thought, but frees us from death, brings forth a new life in our hearts, and is a work of the Holy Spirit. Therefore, this cannot exist with mortal sin, but whenever it appears it brings forth good fruits.[34]

If the Holy Spirit brings a person to faith through the hearing of the Gospel, their life will be changed.

On the other side of the spectrum there is the view taught by many Protestant groups called "eternal security," or 'once saved, always saved." Those who come to faith in Jesus and are saved, regardless of what they do, they cannot be "unsaved."

This is contrary to Scripture. The Bible teaches us to walk carefully in this world because the devil is a roaring lion, seeking whom he might devour (1 Peter 5:8). In Matthew 13, Jesus tells the parable of the sower and the seed. The seed is the Word of God. Some of the seed falls on rocky soil. The seed does sprout, but since there is no water to sustain it, it withers and dies. Some of the seed fall among weeds. It sprouts but is choked by the weeds and dies.

There is no doubt that the Bible teaches that a person can fall away and reject Jesus.

---

[34] Tappert, *Book of Concord*, p. 116:64

Because you board a plane and the pilot knows the way, there is still the remote possibility that the plane will crash, and you won't reach your destination.

The Bible says in Philippians 2:2-13: "Continue to work out your salvation with fear and trembling, for it is God who works in you to will and to act in order to fulfill his good purpose."

Here you have a combination of caution and assurance. We walk carefully in this world knowing that the devil, the world and our sinful nature are always trying to pull us away from Jesus, but we are assured that we are not doing so alone. God is at work in us to fulfill His will and purposes.

The assurance of our eternal salvation is not based on some doctrine of eternal security but on the Word and promises of God. If we grow lazy and careless in our relationship with the Lord, we need to hear the many warnings in God's Word.

But we live by the promises of God.

We read in Philippians 1:6: "Being confident of this, that he who began a good work in you will carry it on to completion until the day of Christ Jesus."

Jesus says regarding His sheep in John 10:28: "I give them eternal life, and they will never perish. No one can snatch them out of My hand."

The Apostle Paul writes in Romans 8:38-39: "For I am convinced that neither death nor life, neither angels nor demons neither the present nor the future, nor any powers, neither height nor depth, nor anything else in all creation, will be able to separate us from the love of God that is in Christ Jesus our Lord.

Settle in your heart: Because of the blood and righteousness of Jesus Christ, you have eternal life in heaven.

The Joy of Heaven

As I get older, in the words of *Mercy Me,* the popular Christian singing group, *I Can Only Imagine* what the joys of heaven will be like. Jesus has provided for us the means for living in joy and peace each day and assurance of a glorious eternal future with Him in heaven.

The Apostle Paul writes in Corinthians 2:9: "What no eye has seen, what no ear has heard, and what no human mind has conceived" -- the things God has prepared for those who love him."

~ ~ ~ ~

Questions for Discussion:

1. Would a local congregation be different if people came to church *because* they were

146

going to heaven rather than *in order to* get to heaven?

2. What does it mean to say, "I don't believe in a *doctrine* of eternal security, rather, I believe in the *promises of God*?"

3. The Apostle writes in Ephesians 2:6: "God raised us up with Christ and seated us with him in the heavenly realms in Christ Jesus." Technically, by position and by virtue of the Ascension of Jesus, we are already seated in the heavenly place. When we die, our *position* will become our *possession*. Discuss it.

!

Conclusion:
Your sins are forgiven!
You have the perfect righteousness
of Jesus Christ!
You are going to heaven
when you die.
You are a forgiven, redeemed,
justified and reconciled saint.
Now, serve the Lord and your
neighbor with joy!

Made in the USA
Monee, IL
02 August 2023